The Vicars of Wells:

A History of the College of Vicars Choral

Anne Crawford

Close Publications

The Vicars of Wells
A History of the College of Vicars Choral
by Anne Crawford

First published 2016
by Close Publications
Wells, Somerset, UK

Layout by Iain MacLeod-Jones
www.imjdesign.co.uk

Printed by St Andrew's Press of Wells

Whilst every effort has been made to trace the owners of the copyright material reproduced herein, the publishers would like to apologise for any omissions and will be pleased to incorporate any missing acknowledgements in future editions.

A CIP catalogue record of this book is available from the British Library

ISBN: 978-0-9572393-6-4

Front Cover image: The Vicars' Painting [detail] (Photograph by Iain MacLeod-Jones)
Back Cover image: Vicars' Close Restored. Lithograph of a mid 19th-century drawing by
F T Dollman (1812–1900) (Photograph by Richard Neale)

THE VICARS OF WELLS:
A HISTORY OF THE VICARS CHORAL

CONTENTS

Chapter 1: Beginnings   1

Chapter 2: The Foundation of the College   14

Chapter 3: To the Reformation and Beyond   30

Chapter 4: Revolution and Restoration   50

Chapter 5: Stagnation and Complacency?   67

Chapter 6: Reform and Revival   81

Chapter 7: Continuity and Change   103

Appendix 1: The Vicars' Oath   116

Appendix 2: The Vicars' Painting   117

Appendix 3: The Payment of Vicars   119

Appendix 4: The Claver Morris Lawsuit   124

Notes   127

Bibliography   137

Index   141

CHAPTER ONE
BEGINNINGS

If you visit Wells Cathedral today and attend a service of choral evensong on one of the days when the men of the choir are singing without the choristers, it is possible, if the music chosen for that day includes plainsong, to sit in the Quire with eyes closed and be transported back through the centuries. The vicars choral of Wells are, and always have been, the singing men of the cathedral choir. The earliest documentary reference to the vicars dates from the late twelfth century, but they were an important part of the cathedral community long before that. In order to understand what that part was, it is necessary to recount a little of the early history of the cathedral itself.

The cathedral church of St Andrew began life as an Anglo-Saxon minster, founded in about 705 A.D. by King Ine of Wessex next to the site of a holy well at the foot of the Mendip Hills, where there had been a place of worship, not necessarily Christian, since the days of the Romano-British. The mission of the new minster within the diocese of Sherborne was to reach out west, into an area where there was as yet no parish organisation. In 909 A.D. it became the cathedral of the newly formed diocese for Somerset. By this stage its main purpose was the perpetual celebration of the liturgy, so that when the seat of the bishop was moved from Wells to Bath in 1088, the life of its clergy changed little. The vision of Bishop Reginald de Bohun to build a new church at Wells to replace the Anglo-Saxon one began to take shape in the 1170s. The whole architecture of the new church, with its quire, nave and aisles was designed for the accommodation of the liturgy. The magnificence of the new building made it entirely appropriate that it should, in 1245, once again become the cathedral church of the newly renamed diocese of Bath and Wells.

At this period there were two types of cathedrals in England, monastic and secular. In the former, the cathedral church was also the abbey church and the monks lived a fully communal life, with the bishop also serving as abbot. At secular cathedrals, the clergy had their own houses and, unlike monks, could own and dispose of property. There were nine secular cathedrals: Chichester, Exeter, Hereford, Lichfield, Lincoln, London (St Paul's), Salisbury, Wells and York. These derived their liturgy and constitution from Norman models, although there was some continuity from Anglo-Saxon traditions, melding into a particular English form, settled at the end of the eleventh century by Archbishop Lanfranc. He issued his 'Decreta pro Ordine S. Benedicti' for the use of monasteries, but he began it with rules for the liturgy which were equally valid for secular churches. This Ordinal defined the character, content and method of services. A little later, in about 1210, Bishop Richard Poore of Salisbury drew up a customary for his cathedral church and this Sarum Customary became the most important and most copied of the customals for secular churches. A customal dealt with the ceremonial of the celebration of the rite, setting out the order of seating in the stalls of the quire, the rules of deportment, and the duties and procedures of those who performed the services of the church year. Exactly when Wells began following the Sarum Use is not recorded, but in 1241 Chapter ordered the correction of the existing Ordinal and did so again in 1273 and 1298; in other words it was being regularly corrected and updated to make the organisation of the services more efficient.[1]

The most senior clergy of the cathedral were then, as now, the canons. Bishop Robert of Lewes (1136-1166) re-founded the Chapter (the governing body) of the church and gave it a constitution based on that of Salisbury, even though at this date the seat of his bishopric was at Bath. He provided for twenty-two canons or prebendaries, each of them financially supported by a small estate, or prebend, granted from among the Chapter or episcopal estates or donated by pious laymen or women. However, the increase in the Chapter's property, particularly in the thirteenth century, led to an increase in both in the number of canons and of the lesser clergy, as it did to the building of the Chapter House (completed c. 1306) in which cathedral business could be conducted. The Chapter House has 51 stalls (one for the bishop) and this was more or less the highest number of canons during the Middle Ages. In the two centuries leading up to the Reformation the number of canons slowly declined; Wells was not one of the wealthiest cathedrals and if money was needed for a major project such as the repair of the fabric, the only way it could be funded was by leaving canonries vacant, using the income from the prebend for repairs and saving on the salary of a vicar.

The canons elected the dean or president of the Chapter from among themselves, but his appointment had to be confirmed by the bishop. The dean was responsible for the cure of souls of all the clergy at Wells, but there were three other dignitaries among the canons who were appointed by the bishop and who were each in charge of a different branch of the administration. In order of precedence they were the precentor, who was responsible for the liturgy and music, the chancellor, who acted as secretary to the Chapter, kept its seals, supervised the schools of grammar and theology and arranged the reading of lessons and sermons, and the treasurer, who guarded the cathedral treasures and provided lights and materials for the services.

The four dignitaries, the 'quatuor personae', as they were known, were the rocks on which the cathedral's spiritual and material welfare was based. They, together with two deputies, the sub-dean and the succentor, were bound to be priests and, unlike the other canons, were not permitted to hold other offices with the cure of souls.[2] Their office, in theory at least, required continuous residence. Initially it was intended that all canons should reside at Wells for a minimum of six months p.a., thus qualifying each canon for a share in the distribution of commons (food and money) after the claims of the dignitaries had been satisfied. For this it was necessary to maintain a prebendal house in Wells and keep household there (a heavy expense). Canons often had other calls on their time, like service to bishop or king for which the canonry had been a reward in the first place, so it gradually became established practice to elect and formally admit a number of the canons to residency in Wells, while the remainder were non-resident. Out of about 40 canons, there were usually between 11-20 resident. For non-resident canons their only connection was a stall in the quire and a voice in Chapter which they rarely bothered to use. Sometimes even residentiary canons were absent on Chapter or episcopal business, or overseeing their own prebendal estate. The number of canons attending services at any one time was therefore small, even though they were the men who were supposed to lead the continuous round of the liturgy. Their households therefore contained at least one member of the lesser clergy who could remain in Wells and perform their liturgical duties for them. These men were known as 'vicars'; the word means deputy. Since the main duty of these vicars was to sing the services, they later became known as 'vicars choral'.[3] Strictly speaking, it was necessary only for these men to be in minor orders, or deacons, but most progressed in time to full priesthood. This system of vicars deputising for canons was certainly in existence by 1140, the date of the earliest extant cathedral statutes.

The canonical hours which the cathedral clergy celebrated each day were: Prime, Terce, Sext, None, Vespers and Compline (the daytime hours) and Matins and Lauds (the night-time hours). The exact form of the service depended on whether it took place on a weekday or Sunday, or a greater or lesser feast day, but there were elements common to all services: the opening sentences, hymn, psalm with antiphon, lesson, hymn and canticle with antiphon. In addition to the hours, mass was celebrated several times a day depending on the number of altars and chantries in use. A vicar's singing duties, therefore, were more or less fulltime, particularly if he had become a priest. The Sarum Customary set out the general rules to be followed for deportment and precedence during these services, which were all held in the quire. The arrangement of the stalls in the quire was of particular importance.[4] There were three rows of seats or stalls: *gradus superior; secunda forma*, and the lowest, the *prima forma*. In secular cathedrals there were return stalls at the west end, against the choir screen and facing the altar. In the nearest stalls to the quire door on the south side sat the dean and on the north side, the precentor; hence the south side (*decani*) had precedence over the north (*cantoris*). In the corners at the east end were the stalls of the chancellor and treasurer. This seating arrangement still continues at Wells.

Next to the four principal canons were the stalls of archdeacons and the abbots of monasteries who held prebends. The sub-dean sat on the *decani* side and the subcentor on the *cantoris*, while the remaining stalls were filled by the canons or their vicars choral. In the *secunda forma* sat the deacons and other clerks, while the *prima forma* was taken by the choristers. In the weekly assignment of the duties of singing and reading, the sides of the choir alternated in being the 'duty' or leading side, so a *decani* week was followed by a *cantoris* one. This alternation was daily over Christmas, Easter and Whitsuntide. From the general body of singers smaller groups were taken out at various times to act as 'rulers of the choir' or to sing certain parts of the service. These either assisted the precentor or acted in his place. For major feasts there were four rulers, and on the most important ones, all four rulers were canons; on others, two were from the senior stalls, ie. canons, and two assistants from the second tier. The chief function of the ruler, besides beginning the responses and singing solo parts, was to discover from the precentor the beginnings of the antiphons and responses and who was to sing them, and where from; this could be the stalls, mid-quire, quire step, pulpitum or mid-altar, as laid down by the customary. While the assignment of singing duties was made by the precentor, those of reading were made by the chancellor.[5] Despite the importance of singing in the daily routine of the cathedral, the earliest reference to an organ comes in 1310, when timber was ordered to build the gallery on which it was to stand. The two large stone corbels on the south side of the nave in the fourth bay just below triforium level are generally believed to have supported the gallery. The organ was probably removed to the pulpitum in about 1335, when the latter was built, a position it has retained ever since. There is also evidence for a second, smaller organ in the Lady Chapel.[6]

Whether the senior members of the communities of clergy who staffed the Anglo-Saxon cathedrals ever employed more junior clerks to sing the services on their behalf on a systematic basis will probably never be known.

Only after the Norman Conquest and the introduction of more complex organisational structures did vicars clearly come to play an essential role. The initial introduction of vicars to sing the services differed from cathedral to cathedral. The early view at Salisbury, sent in response to an enquiry by Reginald de Bohun, Bishop of Bath (1175-1191) on behalf of Wells, was that all canons ought to have vicars except those at schools or travelling to Rome on Chapter business, which meant that even canons in residence and thus able to play their own liturgical parts, were expected to have them. Bishop Joselin (1206-1242) is believed to have ordained vicars at Wells for all prebendaries except three.[7] A vicar could represent his canon only for some of the duties during services. He could take his master's place as *rector chori*, ruling the singing or ministering at the altar, if the canon was resident, but the latter was expected to serve in person on important feast days, and no vicar was supposed to celebrate mass at the high altar unless there was no canon present. Nor could vicars attend Chapter meetings or Chapter business as substitutes for their canons.

In the early 12th century the common funds of the church of St Andrew were insufficient to maintain large numbers of minor clergy or *ministri inferiores* as they were technically known, so each canon was ordered to maintain his vicar personally. This meant that each vicar had personal ties with one of the canons who paid all or part of his stipend, sometimes in the form of maintenance in his household. It also meant that a canon had the right to choose his vicar, although his choice had to be approved by the Chapter. This was a useful form of patronage and could be used to provide for a relative or son of a friend or a tenant. It was also a jealously guarded right. In 1245, after one of the vicars had entered a hospital order in Bruges, the bishop filled the place with his own nominee. An immediate protest by the Dean and Chapter led him to back down and agree that his nominee should be removed and the place filled by the Chapter.[8] Although he might live in the household of a canon, a vicar was not subject to his direction but to that of the Chapter and to the precentor in particular. All vicarial candidates had to be at least in minor orders and from 1278, according to statutes set forth by the Dean and Chapter, underwent some form of musical examination; they could be rejected if their singing voice was unsatisfactory. They then had to serve a probationary year during which they had to learn by heart the psalter, antiphony, hymnary and could only be appointed to a permanent position after a second examination. These rules continued until the Reformation and beyond.[9]

The care with which vicars were chosen indicates their liturgical importance. Some may already have served as choristers and then spent the interim years after their voices had broken and before they were old enough to take orders as 'altarists', assisting the clergy at a specific altar, where they served daily in their choir habits. The altarists were also expected to be present in the quire for the main services on greater feast days and to say the whole psalter daily. For this they received 4d. per week at Wells, paid from the common fund. It was at this point in their lives that they attended the cathedral's Grammar School. A schoolmaster was employed (the first to be noted was Peter of Winchester in c.1180), and in the late 15th century a school hall was built for them over the West Cloister. The Grammar School took in boys from the town as well, and was separate from the Choristers' School, which instructed younger boys, particularly in music although they may also have attended some lessons in the Grammar School. The two did not combine until the 16th century. Research into the origins of the minor clergy at English secular cathedrals is sparse: Nicholas Orme's work on those of Exeter reveals that the majority came from the south-west, and could thus be classed as relatively local, and while some were undoubtedly junior relations of canons or local gentlemen, others may have been the sons of tenants of canonical or Chapter property or parishioners of its benefices, or of Exeter citizens. However, recent work by A.J. Scrase on Wells vicars reveals a surprisingly different pattern. Just over half of those identified as vicars (147) came from Somerset, only a handful from Wells itself. Gloucestershire provided the next largest intake, but others came from as many as twenty other counties, including places as far away as Lincolnshire and Nottinghamshire. Scrase gives a number of possible reasons for this. Wells had a comparatively large number of canons. Some of these were appointed as a result of patronage by the bishop or dean, who would naturally tend to favour kin or people from their own home area. In some cases, relatives followed canons or vicars to Wells and established themselves there for several generations. Whatever their origins, all vicarial candidates were required to be able to read and sing the Latin of the liturgy.[10]

Although vicars were initially accepted while in minor, or deacon's, orders, they were expected to go on and take full orders when they were old enough, the canonical age for which was 30. This meant that there were a group of young vicars between the age of 22 (when they could first take minor orders) and 30 in sub-deacon and deacon's orders, while the majority of older vicars were priests. To be a priest opened up a career path other than singing, for they could either be appointed to a benefice or if they remained vicars they could increase their income by performing extra duties within the cathedral. If they chose not to go on to take full orders, vicars might hope to transfer to a good lay job, since they were literate, and the quality of their voices sometimes led to work in the private households of the wealthy. Having been appointed, a vicar had then to be paid. The income of individual vicars varied somewhat since it came from a number of different sources; this is dealt with in more detail in Appendix 3.

One major addition to a vicar's stipend was the income from obits, or prayers for the souls of the departed, to speed their journey through Purgatory. In the later Middle Ages, increasing numbers of clergy and pious laymen left money or charges on their estate for obits to be said in the cathedral. If the obit took the form of a daily, weekly or annual mass, then the priest saying the mass, one of the minor clergy, was paid to do so, and in some cases, other vicars who attended received extra payments. The priests became known as 'cantarists' or chantry priests. On occasion it was specified that the chantry priest should be a vicar: in 1301, when Bishop William de Marchia (1293-1302) presented the church of Chilterne to Bruton Priory, he reserved payment of 12 marks p.a. to Wells, 5 marks of which was to pay a chaplain to say daily mass at the altar of St Nicholas in the chapel of the Virgin in the cloister, the chaplain to be elected by the vicars from their number. Since the time of Bishop Jocelin, the Lady Chapel off the Cloisters had been staffed by vicars; originally thirteen of them were to sing mass, three of whom were to be priests. The most senior of the three came to be known as the prior of the Chapel. On other occasions, vicars were specifically excluded: in 1306 as part of the major setting up of obits for King Edward I, his two queens and other members of his family, 10 marks p.a. was to be paid to two chaplains (who were not to be vicars) to say 2 masses daily and services for the dead at the altars of St Mary and St Andrew by the entrance to the quire.[11]

If a canon was resident in Wells, then his house provided board and lodging for his vicar. If he was not resident, then the vicar had to find his own accommodation and this usually meant lodgings somewhere in the town. The authorities were aware of the temptations to which this might expose him. In 1243 it was decreed in Chapter that no vicar should live on his own, but there must be at least two of them in one house, so that they could encourage each other to live a virtuous life. Vicars who currently lived alone had until the forthcoming Michaelmas to change their arrangements; if they failed then they would not be permitted to enter the quire and would therefore forfeit their commons (their allowance in lieu of bread and any division of general funds between the vicars when they were in attendance at special services) until such time as the Chapter deemed their arrangements satisfactory. In the following decades the statute was re-issued on a number of occasions, usually after individual vicars had had to be disciplined either for incontinence (the term used for any sexual misbehaviour), quarrelling or other unseemly behaviour.[12] Gradually more and more vicars were accommodated in Chapter property, particularly that granted to the cathedral to fund obits. At an unspecified date before 1284, the Dean and Chapter granted to the vicar Walter Burnel several houses near Monteroy for a rent of 6s. 8d. (half a mark) to be paid to the communar (the financial accounting officer) towards the obit of Luke and Alice Buche. Walter was then free to sub-let the houses to fellow vicars. In the early decades of the 14th century there are plenty of examples of vicars moving between houses owned by the Chapter. A survey of its property in 1316 shows nine houses occupied by vicars.[13]

Despite the best efforts of the Chapter to ensure that vicars shared accommodation and thus kept an eye on each other, it was inevitable that a large group of young men, most only in minor orders, should find chastity difficult to maintain. The 1243 decree is one of the first references to the problem and the Chapter were quite specific. Those who had concubines and children by them were forbidden to allow the mothers to come to their lodgings on the pretence of bringing children for a visit, nor were the vicars to attend feasts where the said women would be present. They were only permitted to converse with them in public before witnesses who were not suspect. Some of the earliest named vicars enter the records because they were disciplined and the records offer a glimpse into the private life of these men. Throughout the late thirteenth and early fourteenth centuries there were a steady stream of cases against named vicars for sexual misdemeanours, often with a partner identified.

In 1244, the year following the decree, John de Cerde was accused of adultery with Avice, wife of David the tanner, who was away on a pilgrimage to the Holy Land. John confessed his guilt and submitted to the future loss of his vicarage should any scandal arise from this or any other fault. Whether or not there was any public scandal tended to tip the balance as far as punishment went. In 1248 the vicar William de Hoyland was charged with incontinence with the daughter of Josce. It was reported that on the night of the feast of St John the Baptist he was seen carrying his shoes in his hands the next morning in Baggelegh Wood, Wedmore, and was also charged with violence against the said Josce. Like John, William confessed to the Chapter, but because in this case there was a public scandal, it was decreed that until the forthcoming feast of the Nativity of the Virgin, William should suffer the humiliation of sitting with the boy choristers on their bench, and if he repeated his offence he would lose his vicarage. This was not an idle threat. In 1251, Geoffrey de Tottensis applied for the restoration of his vicarage after he had been deprived for 3 years. This was probably for a second offence because he had been accused of adultery in 1244.[14] The records do not tell us whether he was re-instated, but in 1262, another deprived vicar, Geffrey de Praule, craved restoration of his vicarage, currently held by Ralph, son of a painter, or a benefice of similar value. The Chapter promised to collate him to the next vicarage in their gift or would approve if any canon chose to appoint him. To be fair to the vicars, they were not the only ones who found chastity hard to maintain. In 1257 a canon was condemned for incontinence and deprived of his prebend for a year; the profit of 8 marks p.a. went to the fabric fund.[15]

It is difficult to know what happened to individual vicars during a period of deprivation; did they live off the charity of their friends, return to their families, or earn their living in some other sort of way? Voluntary resignation from a secure, lifelong post was rare, but did sometimes occur. Luke de Harptree was given licence by the Dean and Chapter in 1323 to visit the holy places on pilgrimage and return to his vicarage provided he find a substitute in the meantime and they made a formal declaration that he had not been suspended, excommunicated or detected in crime. Harptree was in fact reaping the reward for his diligence in the Chapter's service; three years previously he had been appointed as their escheator, proctor and special attorney to take possession of the profits of prebends vacant by death, which by ancient custom belonged to the Chapter for the first year of vacancy.[16] Both bishops and the Chapter found it very useful to delegate business to specific vicars, most of them from the ranks of those seniors who were priests and some of them seem to have spent their careers in administration. It was a good route to promotion. In 1320, for instance, Richard de Pencriz was rewarded with the incumbency of St Cuthbert's, the parish church of Wells, after he had been in post as sub-treasurer for some years. In 1329 Walter de Hulle was permitted by dispensation of the Dean and Chapter, for his diligence in their service, to take the profits of his vicarage without being bound to know the divine service or to perform his duties in residence, though such profits excluded the daily distributions of food and those for the anniversaries of the dead. Hulle was one of eight vicars between 1250 and 1500 who rose from the ranks of vicars to become a canon, the final prize for an ambitious and competent vicar. Some, like John Brether in 1259, left to pursue their studies, stating that he voluntarily resigned his vicarage in order to 'study in the schools and while youth remained, to perfect himself in literature'.[17]

A set of statutes promulgated by Dean Water de Haselchawe and the Chapter in 1298 included many that relate to the vicars and illuminate aspects of their lives at the end of the thirteenth century.[18] All vicars were expected to be present every day for the offices of Matins, Prime, Evensong and Compline, but for Terce, Sext and None, it was sufficient if there were six on each side of the choir, so the vicars probably worked out an informal rota. It was noted that certain vicars left the quire during divine service to gossip with lay persons of doubtful reputation in the nave and behind pillars, ostensibly to buy goods exposed there for sale. To put an end to this scandal, no vicar in future was to be permitted to leave the quire until the office was over. The buying and selling of goods in the nave was also strictly forbidden, while the vicars were not permitted to go to the market place or the meat and fish stalls in their choir habits, but neither were they to appear in the church without them after the last bell had sounded. Every vicar was to go daily to see if he or his canon was scheduled to perform any office, particularly ruling the choir. The statutes stated that the ruler had to ensure he knew how to begin the hymns and all the chants and how to start the psalms in the right mode lest on account of his error, discord should arise in the choir. If anyone was culpably in error he would lose his stipend for the day. The singing in the choir must be even and no one was to go faster than his neighbour and all should listen carefully at the pauses. There were further regulations about wearing their silk copes on greater feast days, attending the reading of the lesson in the Chapter House after Prime, and not attending the Office of the Dead solely on days when there was to be a distribution of money, nor of shirking their duties as chantry chaplains; the latter bore the penalty of a fine of one penny for each lapse.

As far as the Statutes related to the vicars' personal lives, the earlier rules about not living on their own, and not keeping concubines were reiterated and because both vicars and canons sometimes refused to live in their allotted houses due to dilapidation or missing furniture, Chapter would in future appoint two overseers to inspect the houses at Easter each year and assess dilapidations, all of which were to be put right by the following Michaelmas. A further set of statutes dating from 1331 emphasised that it was for canons to decide whether their vicars were to live and eat with them or not. It is from this set that we learn that the cathedral clergy were in the habit of putting on theatrical displays between the feast of Christmas and the octave of Holy Innocents Day, introducing dressed up figures into the church, there to exercise silly pranks and gesticulations. Since this was utterly opposed to clerical decency, hindered divine service and was forbidden by church rules, it was ordered to cease at once. This expression of outrage might have carried more weight if Dean John Godelee had not been in office and presumably aware of the custom, for the previous quarter century. On whether or not this statute was obeyed the records are silent, but since the statute was re-issued seven years later, presumably not.[19]

That the 1331 cathedral statutes were only an interim measure is made clear by a major set promulgated in 1338. While most of the sets previously discussed were issued by the Dean and Chapter 'in the time of' whoever held the deanery, the 1338 set specifically state that they were issued in the time of Bishop Ralph of Shrewsbury and made at his request. A great many of them concerned the vicars. Regular note was to be taken of those absent from services and report made weekly to Chapter, and several more set out the level of attendance, the clothing, correct tonsure, punctuality and behaviour during services expected of them. The laws relating to their admission and probation were reiterated in some detail and it was made clear that no vicar during his year of probation was to stand in the highest grade or sing the High Mass at the High Altar on pain of suspension. No vicar, chorister or altarist was to read a lesson, epistle or gospel, without first having been heard so that mistakes in '*accentu, dictione vel sillaba*' might be avoided. The statutes then moved on to cover the personal lives of the vicars, which 'gravely perturbed' the Dean and Chapter. Many went hunting, fowling and fishing, cared nothing for their clerical estate and took part in dances and masques, prowling the streets of the city leading a riotous existence, singing and shouting and discrediting the office of the clergy and causing scandal to the people. In future anyone caught behaving thus would be suspended for two months and for a second offence, 'the Church of Wells shall have nothing more to do with him'. Others were in the habit of frequenting alehouses, playing backgammon and generally conducting themselves in a highly unbefitting manner, all of which was to be severely punished in the future. It had even come to the ears of the Chapter that certain vicars were in the habit of taking part in drinking bouts in which 'all oblige themselves to drink the same amount and he who makes the most drunk and drinks the longest cups himself earned the greatest praise'. Others were guilty of carrying swords and inflicting grievous bodily harm on others and even committing heinous sacrilege (unspecified, but presumably committing such crimes in the cathedral itself). If any vicar left anything to his concubine in his will, such a bequest should be applied to the fabric of the cathedral instead. Given that in 1338 there were approximately forty to fifty vicars, even if only one or two were guilty of each of the crimes specified, or there were several guilty of all of them, then clearly the control of the Chapter over the vicars had slipped way below the level of acceptability.[20]

Part of the problems thus identified was the failure to control the living arrangements of the vicars. Attempts to regulate them had not been completely successful, and by this date the Dean and Chapter had already been considering how to provide communal living quarters for the vicars. By 1300 York, Lincoln and St. Paul's already had some form of residential accommodation for their vicars; at York, for instance, the vicars had a communal hall and dormitory by the mid 13th century, their corporate body recognised by the archbishop and dean and chapter. Since at the start of the fourteenth century there were about fifty vicars choral at Wells it was clearly going to be a major undertaking to provide them with accommodation.[21] The custom of leasing empty Chapter-owned houses to a group of vicars was a reasonably successful halfway measure; the next step was to provide something purpose built. At a special Chapter meeting, undated but c. 1318-23, it was noted that a previous decision 'that houses shall be built for the vicars to live together' had been taken but not implemented. Under Dean John Godelee (1305-1333), a site had been agreed by Chapter. It was to stretch from the canonical house of Sir William de Cherlton to 'the penthouse where the masons work' and part of the churchyard there might be taken for the house and grounds 'for the recreation of the inhabitants'. It was also proposed that if the Dean saw fit to take on himself the building costs, he might settle the first year's rent for the good of his soul in the church as he saw fit.[22] Although the site cannot be identified for certain, it seems highly likely that the canonical house was that now known as 'The Rib'; this, with part of the Camery, which had already been set aside as a burial ground for the vicars, and easy access to the Lady Chapel-by-the-Cloister, which was already staffed by the vicars, would have been a highly suitable location for communal accommodation.

For reasons unknown, this scheme, too, was abandoned. It was followed in 1332 by one for a parcel of land at the western end of Cathedral Green, then used for burials, parallel to Sadler Street. Chapter granted to Dean Godelee and his brother Canon Hamelin de Godelee a plot 'within the churchyard next to the highway on the west side of the said churchyard, lying between the churchyard wall on the north and the other churchyard wall on the south churchyard'.[23] Both these schemes for accommodation for the vicars seem to have closely involved Dean Godelee, and on his death within less than a year the second scheme, too, came to nothing. If either had come to fruition, initiated by a dean and built on the Cathedral's own land, then the history of the vicars choral of Wells might have taken a different course. As it was, by the time the new statutes were issued under the aegis of Bishop Ralph, the problem was becoming increasingly urgent.

CHAPTER TWO
THE FOUNDATION OF THE COLLEGE

The collapse of the Chapter's plans for the accommodation of the vicars under Dean Godelee was followed by fifteen years of inactivity, and then Bishop Ralph of Shrewsbury (1329-1363) decided to take a direct interest. As befitted his status, his scheme was considerably more ambitious. Exactly when his plans began to take shape is difficult to determine, but they were probably a result of concerns expressed in the statutes of 1338 and they were well under way by 3 December 1348. On that day King Edward III issued to Bishop Ralph a licence 'in mortmain' – permission to permanently alienate to a collegiate organisation lands which would henceforth be exempt from feudal dues. The licence permitted him to assign to the vicars of Wells 'a certain place of the soil of the church of St Andrew in Wells, and of the Bishop in the same place, which was lately collated by the Bishop of the same place upon Master Alan de Hotham, Canon of that church, for his habitation, and the houses in the same place by the said Ralph built and to be built. To have and to hold to them, and their successor vicars of the church aforesaid for their common and perpetual habitation'. The bishop was also permitted to charge his lands at Congresbury and Wookey with an annuity of ten pounds as an endowment for the vicars. Three weeks later, on 30 December, Bishop Ralph incorporated the College of Vicars Choral at Wells by charter; they were the first group of vicars to be thus formally incorporated in the country.[1]

Both the royal licence and the vicars' charter were a confirmation of an earlier grant by Bishop Ralph, which does not survive, but which may have been as early as 1345. The canonical house of Adam de Hotham was one of a number in the bishop's own gift and the Chapter had no control over who held them. It was very conveniently situated almost opposite the north door of the cathedral and its grounds stretched northwards as far as the road known as the North Liberty. It was one of a row of similar houses with long gardens on that side of Cathedral Green. The dimensions of the plot, long and narrow as it was, dictated the shape of what was to become known for centuries as the New Close and more recently as Vicars' Close. Adam de Hotham had been collated to the house in 1328 and is known to have been in Somerset in 1344, but by 1350 he was in London acting as official receiver of monies to be collected for the papal nuncio. He naturally retained his prebend and its income, but was inevitably non-resident and no longer had need of his canonical house. The house as it stood may have been initially used by the vicars for their common purposes, in which case the first part of the building works were the erection of individual houses for them.[2] It has also been suggested that, conversely, the hall was the first part to be built and the vicars may have used it as a dormitory while the rest of the buildings were completed. The hall itself, at first floor level, was almost certainly built over what had been the hall of the canonical house, one end of which may have served as a chapel for the vicars; some thirteenth century features of de Hotham's hall survive.

Several of the original fittings of the new hall can also still be seen in situ. The glass in the tracery lights of the original windows is probably contemporary with the building and shows St. Margaret in the south window and St. Katherine in the north one, with possibly St. Hugh in the adjacent one. Others are the two remarkable wooden figures on the east wall. Still with some paint visible, and standing on half-columnar corbels, the two were clearly made as a pair. They have usually been taken to represent the Annunciation, but another possible identification is a Visitation group of the Virgin Mary and her cousin Elizabeth, mother of John the Baptist. They were carved in the early 1360s and if there was originally a chapel beneath the hall, would probably have been placed there. If that was demolished to widen the gateway to the Close in the 1460s, that is probably when the figures moved to the position they still occupy, above what would have been the site of the hall's high table.[3] The large bread cupboard, designed to hold the daily bread rations of all forty-two vicars, battered and worn, but still intact is also contemporary with the building and the long benches probably date from then as well. Adjoining the hall to the west is the buttery or kitchen, its fireplace on the west wall still with its spit in place, and the original stone sink, carved from a single block of stone, with the drain running north/south on the floor to a chute fixed in a hole in the wall, where the water could flow out. Beneath the kitchen there was probably a bakehouse and a brewhouse.

Whatever the exact order of the building work, by the end of 1348 when the college was incorporated, Bishop Ralph could declare in his charter that he was handing over, not only the site, but 'the houses in the same place, now new by us built and to be built' and the Hall, kitchen and bakehouse for their common use. The speed at which the building work was undertaken was particularly fortunate because in the autumn of 1348 the Black Death reached the south-west. When he granted his charter, Bishop Ralph dated it from Wiveliscombe, a rural manor from which he directed the affairs of his diocese throughout the period of the plague. He was wise to do so: 47.6% of the clergy in the diocese died in the winter of 1348/9 and among the general population of Somerset, the death rate was between a third and a half. This would inevitably have brought any uncompleted building work to a temporary halt.

There is independent evidence that the hall was finished by 1348. It comes from the will of a Bristol widow, Alice Swansee, drawn up on 7 November after the death of her son Philip, a Wells vicar choral; both of them may well have died of the plague. Alice requested that she be buried, not in Bristol, but at Wells near her son, in the Palm churchyard, which was normally reserved for clergy. To ensure the granting of her request, she bequeathed two silver cups and a maser to the high altar of the cathedral. She then bequeathed 'one brass 32-gallon vessel for the use of the Vicars serving in the said church of St. Andrew and dwelling in the new building which the bishop has erected in the same town; also one better basin with hanging ewer; and a table destined for the Vicars' hall'.[4] This suggests that the hall had only recently been finished, and the vicars were still engaged in furnishing it.

While the hall was a common enough type, the lodgings for the vicars were highly unusual. The two rows of houses, 42 in all, running in parallel north of the hall provided each man with not one, but two chambers. While sets of similar chambers could be found in the early college buildings of Oxford and Cambridge, each set was built above each other round a central communal staircase. At Wells, the two chambers were built one above the other, a ground floor 'hall' with a chamber above, probably with a separate small room, the whole forming a small house with its own internal staircase. While the houses were very similar, they were not uniform, suggesting that several teams of masons were at work. Incorporated into the staircase projection at the rear of each house was a latrine, which discharged into a main drain. A stone drain, now largely filled in, still runs the length of the close on each side, just behind the housing range. Prior to the Reformation, each vicar was required to live singly, though some vicars had servants, and there was no need for individual cooking facilities, since they ate communally, 'living together at meat and drinke att the Common Costs and Expenses'. The unusually generous amount of accommodation has raised the question of whether, in a reversal of former custom, canons living outside Wells resided with their vicars when visiting the cathedral. It is not, however, known whether the canons continued to pay small stipends to their individual vicars after the founding of the college, maintaining the strong personal link which had existed between them. Because the site and the college came as a gift of the bishop, he and his successors had the right to collate new vicars to specific houses in the close. Each vicar had a secure tenancy of his house once he had been collated to it unless he left it for six months without reasonable cause. In recompense for these benefits, Bishop Ralph required that every time a vicar passed from the college to the cathedral he say the Lord's Prayer and the Salutation of the Angel for the bishop and his successors.[5]

An extract from the will of Bishop Ralph, who died in 1363, bequeathed 'to the Vicars of Wells inhabiting the houses built by me, twenty quarters of wheat, twenty quarters of barley, twenty quarters of oats, ten oxen, ten cows and one hundred sheep', thus indicating that the whole was certainly completed in his lifetime.[6] This is confirmed by a grant in December 1355 by Elizabeth, widow of Sir John Wellesley, of all his lands etc at Wellesley near Wells to the vicars 'dwelling in the new work and eating together in their hall', which implies that by that date all construction work was finished and that the close was thought of as a single unit.[7] By becoming the vicars' benefactor both in providing the site from his own holdings and giving them collegiate status, Bishop Ralph had ensured that the new college was independent of the Dean and Chapter. This very independence, however, led to a constant thread of tension running throughout the history of the relations between the two. The Chapter were reliant on the vicars for their singing of the liturgy, but in turn the vicars were dependent on the Chapter for the allowances and fees for the additional services that they sang to augment the small stipend they received; the college endowment was to support their communal life, not add to their personal incomes. The bishop acted as arbitrator in any unresolved disputes between Chapter and college.

Bishop Ralph drew up a series of statutes for the governance of the new college. The original statutes do not survive but they were copied and incorporated into Bishop Thomas Bekynton's statutes of 1459, and these were in turn copied by Dean William Cosyn (1498-1525) in his memoranda book. Bekynton begins his list of statutes with a tribute to the memory of Bishop Ralph and sets out the latter's reasons for building the college. It was to enable the vicars to 'be freer to serve God, live more respectably and nearer the church, attend divine service constantly, and meet together for meals in a companionable way, but without idle and scurrilous gossip.'[8] Bishop Ralph had already dealt with the proper behaviour expected of the vicars in the cathedral in the statutes of 1338 that he encouraged the Chapter to issue (see Chapter 1). It is instructive to note that the first proper statute for the College comprised remedies against those who disrupted college affairs and sowed discord among the vicars. The names of the offenders and their punishment had to be registered; Bekynton noted that the first such register dated from 8 Sept.1394.[9] Only then did the statutes turn to the actual governance of the college. Annually on St Matthew's Day (21 Sept.) a number of officials were to be elected by the vicars from among their number. There were to be two principals, two receivers and three auditors, the duplication of post holders ensuring that no one vicar had a monopoly on power or responsibility or the handling of monies. In addition, five elders were to be elected each year, who, with the officeholders, formed a ruling council. All the offices were honorary. The duties of the principals were to correct all abuses, see that the houses in the Close were kept in repair and ensure that persons of ill repute were kept out of the Close (which primarily meant women). The receivers were responsible for administering all the vicars' property and rendering their accounts to the principals. Each week (commencing one month after his admission) one of the vicars took his turn to act as steward, providing his brethren with their individual allowance of bread and beer and reading the Bible at dinner. Each Friday or Saturday he had to collect the vicars' payment for their commons, ensuring that none received them while his master was in residence, and then render his account; this suggests that while a vicar's canon was in residence, he was expected to eat with him in his house rather than with his fellows in hall. Any vicar who did not pay his bill was to be punished.

Given his care over the details of the governance of the new college, it is hardly surprising that Bishop Ralph was equally specific on the behaviour required of the vicars. This was monitored by the principals, who imposed fines on those who infringed the rules; in many cases even the level of the fine (which varied from one penny to forty) was laid down in the statutes. Vicars were not permitted to keep horses or hounds, make any noise in the Close after the cathedral curfew sounded, and anyone leaving the Close thereafter had to ensure that its gate was closed. The vicars were not to share their houses or entertain women of doubtful reputation, nor have guests who stayed longer than three days, though this rule did not apply to the sick. Naturally any vicar abusing or laying hands on one of his brethren was heavily fined and they were charged with conversing in peaceable and orderly fashion at table and avoiding argument, nor was swearing tolerated. The highest fine, 40 shillings, was reserved for offenders of the rule against two living together, and the second highest, 20 shillings, was reserved for striking any of the college servants. Lest the statutes appear too negative, the collegiate spirit was encouraged by an oath sworn by each new vicar. It makes no mention of the cathedral or the reason for their employment, but encompasses keeping the college statutes, obeying the senior office holders, being discreet about college business and in all being a 'behofull and diligent helper as god me bidys'.[10] There was naturally a penalty for any vicar who revealed the secrets of the Close to any outsider. An annual reading of the statutes, in English, was instituted, so that all the vicars were aware of the rules.

Bishop Ralph had therefore done his best to establish his college as one that would comprise meek, clean-living clerks, without financial worries and with a form of self-government that would ensure all was run as he wished. Unfortunately, things did not turn out quite like that. More efficient living arrangements does not change the nature of young men, and the vicars continued as quarrelsome and sexually incontinent as before. As Bishop Bekynton noted, the first register recording the affairs of the college at the meetings held in hall dates from 1394 and many of the entries relate to disciplinary problems.[11] These were recorded because the main penalties took the form of financial bonds. In general, the first offence was duly noted and the perpetrator forgiven but bound over to pay one of the penalty sums if he offended again. Sometimes even a second offence was forgiven. In one of the earliest cases recorded, John Axminster and John Graye had laid violent hands on each other during a quarrel and were warned that they would pay the Hall penalty without any mitigation if they offended again. The following year angry words were uttered on both sides, but apparently no physical force was used this time. Again, they were only warned not to let it happen again and they exchanged the kiss of peace publicly in the Hall.

In 1410, two of the priest vicars, John Halston and Walter Gybbes had a quarrel which turned violent and at their hearing, John was considered the most to blame and was therefore fined the 6s.8d. imposed on him previously, but Walter had drawn his knife, so was fined 3s.4d. They were both warned that in the event of any future quarrel, they would both pay the maximum fine of 20s. On this occasion the principals took the opportunity to remind the vicars, that the statutory fine for quarrelling and stirring up strife against their fellows was 20s. for each occasion they were found guilty. All the fines that were paid went into the common fund of the Hall. In such a small community as the college, the principals who were enforcing the penalties knew the individuals concerned and the circumstances of the quarrels and judged accordingly in a public meeting. Their decisions, therefore had to be considered just by their fellows. In 1440 a dispute between Thomas German and John Tregodek was discussed before the principals and the fellowship of the common hall until 'at last the truth of this affair having been recognised....it was accepted that the said Thomas German was to blame and deserved to be punished'. If the need to discipline a vicar reached as far as the Chapter, then the case was serious indeed and involved performance of their official duties or their behaviour in the cathedral. In 1360, in Chapter and before nearly all the vicars, the latter were commanded on oath to certify whether Stephen Ferror, a probationer of a year or more, was a fit person to be made a perpetual vicar. After secret deliberation, the vicars certified that although he had knowledge of chanting and reading, he had so borne himself in manners and conditions that he ought to be altogether rejected from his vicarage and not confirmed as a perpetual vicar. With the consent of the canons, he was removed. At least Ferror does not seem to been involved in a violent fight in the cathedral. In October 1372, the Dean and Chapter and a notary public, meeting in 'the audit chamber over a gate on the west side of the cloister' (possibly the gate reopened in 2009), dealt with the case of Philip Erdesleygh and Richard Brere, both of them priest vicars, who had polluted the church through the shedding of blood. The bishop had to be called in to cleanse the church spiritually and the two vicars had until the following Michaelmas to hand over the sum required to cover the expense involved to the communar. [12]

Occasionally there were vicars whose behaviour was so disruptive that it is a wonder that they were never expelled. Richard Hulle first appears in the college register early in the 1390s (the exact date is not clear), when two of the vicars were appointed arbitrators to settle a dispute between him and Simon Urchisfont and John Orum. Their decision was that if Richard uttered any defamatory words or preferred any unjust charges against his two fellows, then he had to pay without any possibility of remission, ten shillings to the Hall receivers. Not only that but the two principals seized the opportunity to rule, with the consent of all the vicars, that if Richard defamed or slandered any of his fellows he would incur the same penalty; if he caused undue noise, quarrel or complaint at the time of dinner or supper, or hindered the readings, he was to be fined 40 pence. At the same time, since he had already been warned about keeping a horse in his house overnight, he was now convicted of the charge and fined 40d. Similarly he had been warned about his manservant – whether this was because his servant had misbehaved or because individual vicars were not permitted to keep servants is not clear – and since he had chosen not to send the man away, he was now fined a further 6d.

All was peaceful for a few months and then in January 1394 Richard was summoned to appear before the Dean and Chapter. The dean put it to him that as a perpetual vicar, he had sworn an oath to uphold the statutes and customs used and approved in the cathedral, which Richard acknowledged. The dean then charged him with frequently disturbing divine service, especially in the Quire and strolling about the pillars of the church (Nave) during divine service and withdrawing from services to gossip with laymen and suspicious persons; that he had let his hair grow and did not use the tonsure as befitted his position and had not taken sub-deacon's orders at the due time, as his vicar's place required. The dean also complained that he did not apply himself with all diligence to the sacred psalter, hymns and antiphonies. Since Richard openly acknowledged that he had committed the faults of which he was charged, he was given a week to show cause why he should not be convicted of perjury, i.e. breaking his vicar's oath. Four days later Richard was back in the Chapter House charged with uttering slanderous and disparaging words about the canons and the vicars in various places in the city and within the cathedral close. He was warned by the dean that if he was ever found guilty of uttering slanderous words about any canon in future, he would be fined 40s. to the Fabric fund, and about any vicar, 13s. 4d., without any remission or postponement. The record is then silent until 1408, when he was found guilty of laying violent hands on the vicar principal, and even then his fine was graciously reduced from 3s.4d. to 12d.[13] Quite why Richard was treated as leniently as he was is a mystery, but suggests that as well as money (witness the horse and servant), he had an influential patron and possibly a particularly fine singing voice.

Occasionally the principals did have recourse to the sanction of expelling a vicar from hall for a set period of time. Not that those expelled always took their punishment too seriously. In 1407 William Boyfield was excluded for 'his various manifest offences' by consent of all his fellows, but the following Sunday re-appeared at dinner-time and said he would by no means stay out of the hall. Since he would not leave, the other vicars present went away for the time being to eat somewhere else themselves. The same thing happened at supper time, and it was not until the following Friday that William repented, submitted himself to the fellowship and asked for pardon, before paying a fine of 3s.4d. Although a cursory glance at the register for the first century of the college's existence gives the impression that much of the business conducted in hall was dealing with quarrels between its members, in fact a couple of dozen such issues in a hundred years hardly seems excessive. Because these incidents shine rare light onto the lives of individual medieval men, it has given rise to the somewhat highly-coloured myth of 'naughty vicars'.

Accounts for the period 1420-25 illustrate the vicars' communal life. They paid two carpenters 6s.8d. for making a dresser for the kitchen, probably from wood from a tree they had just received as a gift; 16s.7d. went on making napery and towels and repairing older ones; 8d. was spent on a gallon of wine, and an apron and gown was purchased for Thomas, their cook. The cook's salary was 26s.8d., while a laundress received 5s.4d. They had a communal garden, for which they paid 11d. for two loads of dung and 14d. for 'leeks plantes' together with 8d. for a man hired for a day and a half to plant them and 2d. for watering them. Nothing in the accounts indicates where this garden was, but in the late 16th century, the vicars' garden, probably the same one, was situated on the east side of Montrey Lane, next to their barton or farmyard, which was generally leased out. As a community, the college benefited from generous gifts. Archbishop Arundel gave it a beautiful flagon with a cover valued at £20 at the end of the 14th century, Canon Robert Perlee a silver cup with a cover, and one of their own, John Hull, 4 silver spoons.[14]

The admirably democratic custom of every vicar taking his weekly turn as steward to issue bread and ale, collecting payment for them at the end of each week sometimes failed to function smoothly. In 1442 the principals were grappling with the tricky problem of vicars who, when it was their turn to act as stewards for the week, delayed paying for the victuals they bought from tradespeople in the town and 'this gave rise to a great scandal not only against those who did not pay, but against the whole body of Vicars'. Earlier problems had arisen when individual vicars did not pay for their battels promptly, but this was the first time, apparently, that the suppliers suffered from late payment. Stewards were supposed to draw up their accounts at the end of the week and ask their fellows for payment, and have the original bills to hand if required. This rule was now re-iterated and they were warned that if they failed in this for more than eight days afterwards, then they were forbidden to make any further request for payment, presumably leaving them to settle bills from their own purse. Furthermore, the stewards were supposed to be on hand from the hour of dinner until curfew to hand out the bread and ale which formed the battels. In 1442 the principals decided that if they received any complaint from a trader about late payment, they would summon both him and the steward at fault before them and settle the matter.[15]

The problems of the office of steward continued to rumble on. In 1465, the executors of Bishop Bekynton made a payment of 100 shillings to the college principals to provide a permanent solution. This was because some of the newest and youngest stewards found it very hard to produce the payment of 40d. asked of each steward as down payment for his week of office. With the lump sum provided as an endowment, in future the steward was to receive

10 shillings from the principals each week to buy victuals and at the end of the week when the money for battels had been collected in, he would refund the advance. On 18 November 1468, the steward of the week, Peter Cashell, found himself in serious trouble over a theft from the store-room, which it was his responsibility to keep locked. The thief or thieves had made off with three ancient mazers (drinking vessels made of wood and often with silver rims) as well as newer ones which had cost 50s. for making and gilding, together with a metal boss, having a picture of St James in the middle and weighing 34 ounces, and 18 spoons each worth 3d. The total haul was valued at £14 0s. 4d. Naturally early suspicion fell on Cashell himself, but he turned detective, 'strove and investigated in various places and at last found out that the thieves had opened various doors and robbed the store-room during the night and sold the cups and spoons in Bristol. Cashell managed to regain possession of the mazers (though apparently not the spoons) and was exonerated of the negligence previously attributed to him.

The degree of slackness that had crept into the vicars' corporate behaviour illustrated above was compounded three years later when the principals noted that 'women of evil and dishonest repute' were present in the hall on feast days for breakfast and drinking'. The scandal that this had given rise to prompted the principals to act, ordaining by common consent that if such persons were found in future in any house of the fellowship, openly or privately, or if any steward was found to have given them food, bread or ale, he should pay for each offence 12d. and after three such warnings he would be sentenced to a penalty at the principals' discretion – an early example of the 'three strikes and you are out' policy. In this case, as in the one concerning battels, it was only the threat of a public scandal that forced the principals into action. On the other hand, when their own authority was questioned, they were quick to impose it. Hall meetings took place after dinner when the vicars met to discuss any matters of interest or concern. On 28 April 1447 such a meeting had been called, but on the day, one of the two principals, John Bekynton, was dining with Canon John Wansford and was late getting back for the meeting. One of the vicars, William Dudcot, protested that the amount of reverence shown to senior vicars, and particularly principals, by the others was wrong, and that it was not fitting for vicars to wait for the principals after the meal but that the latter ought to await the coming of their fellows. These 'disgraceful and truly intemperate words' resulted in Dudcot being ordered out of the hall while his rebellious behaviour was discussed. He refused to go and was immediately excluded from all the commons and profits of the hall until he recognised his fault. He submitted later in the day, acknowledging himself guilty of behaving heedlessly, and was re-admitted to hall, but warned that if he or any other vicar uttered such intemperate words or ideas before the principals or any of their fellows, then the fine would be 6s.8d.[16]

The early years of the fifteenth century saw a number of changes to the physical appearance of the Close, most of them during the episcopate of Bishop Nicholas Bubwith [1407-1424]. First was probably the vicars' desire for the creation of gardens in front of each house, with walls built to mark boundaries. When this was done, each house and garden was given a stone arched gateway, five of which still remain in place. It was this development that turned the Close from a college quadrangle into a street. Sometimes the gardens themselves gave rise to problems. A few decades later (the year is not given), John Cleve found himself in trouble because he initially refused to cut down the bay trees in his garden which were causing annoyance to his fellows; exactly what the problem was is not specified, but in the end Cleve capitulated.[17] A little later, during the 1420s, the administrative block to the rear of the hall went up, made necessary by the slowly increasing accumulation of properties owned by the vicars. Access was via a spiral staircase from the hall and the main room was used as an exchequer, where the receiver, annually elected by the vicars, took in the rents and dues from their estates. It has an elaborated carved oak roof and was well-equipped with a cupboard for writing materials, a fireplace and a small lavabo or wash basin. The windows, unglazed, were fitted with wooden shutters. The exchequer gave access on to a small muniment room in the tower at the end of the block, designed for the storage of the vicars' estate records, complete with a wooden filing cabinet and fitted cupboards. Both these and an oak storage chest in the exchequer survive in situ. From the muniment room a narrow staircase leads down to the vicars' treasury and in the floor of the former, under the floor board, was a concealed iron bar which could be dropped through three staples, one above and one below the door and one in the middle of the door itself, which prevented the treasury door from being opened. On the outside wall of the administrative, or treasury, block is a wide stone covered staircase leading from the Close to the Hall. It is not clear who paid for this building work, since the vicars themselves could not have afforded it, so it may have owed its existence to the generosity of Bishop Bubwith. However, a little later, in 1448, the vicars agreed with the executors of Henry Martyn, the tenant of their house and garden in Moniers Lane, that instead of the repairs due to be made on that property, they would pay for a vault beneath the tower adjoining the staircase and accessed from the muniment room above. Martyn was himself a vicar choral and his executors made good the agreement and provided a treasury complete with up-to-date security and more fitted cupboards in which to store the college valuables.

The final major change to the appearance of the Close was the building of the chapel at the north end. Whether there was an earlier building on the site or whether it was always intended for a chapel when money became available is not known; certainly Bishop Ralph made provision for a special chaplain for the college in 1351 and it is possible that the undercroft of the hall initially provided space for a chapel as well as storerooms. In the past it was sometimes held that the Close chapel was built in the late 14th century, with the upper storey added in the 15th, but archaeological evidence makes it clear that all the building dates from the 15th century. The work probably took place during the episcopates of Bishop Bubwith and Stafford [1425-43] and is generally regarded as having been completed about 1425-30, though the earliest firm documentary reference to the chapel itself is not until 1447. However, in accounts for 1420, payment is recorded for a brass chain hanging before the Coronation of Our Lady, and for a lamp, while an offering of 5s. was made on the day of the Assumption of Our Lady. In 1425 six and a half gallons of oil were purchased to keep the lamp burning before the image of the Coronation of Our Lady, and the man responsible as keeper was paid 12d. This strongly suggests that the chapel was furnished and in use by 1420, even if perhaps the upper storey, which was to become a library for the college, had not been completed before the death of Bishop Bubwith in 1424. Although the payments do not specifically refer to the new chapel, the purchase of furnishings suggest this was not for any former chapel below the hall. In a charter of 1479 the chapel is formally recorded as being dedicated to the Assumption of the Virgin, and at a re-dedication in 1498 St Katherine was added.

The Close was thus finally enclosed, with the only entrance being on the south side. It is not as yet clear when and for what reason, but a late fifteenth century wing was added to No. 14, joining it to the adjacent chapel, and making it much larger than the other houses. At much the same time as the building of the new administrative block, the eastern end of the ground floor of the hall (if it had previously been used as a chapel, it was now redundant) was sacrificed to make two arches into the Close itself. The smaller one was for pedestrians and the larger allowed for the passage of carts from the road outside. The original small pedestrian entrance to the east was then incorporated into the first house in the Close, now 1 St. Andrew's Street. The earliest reference to the 'great gate at the entry of the Close' comes in 1425, when it had a minor repair. A fresh water supply for the Close 'from the spring called Beriall', probably provided by Bishop Bekynton, piped water into each house, with the college contributing 10 marks; remains of the pipes have been found. There may have been a conduit at the top of the close, where a cistern could have provided a gravity feed to take water to the houses as well as up to the first floor kitchen of the hall. The first description of Vicars' Close was given by William Worcestre in 1480 as 'a road built up on both sides ... with the houses of the vicars. 22 houses are built on each side, with very high chimneys and walled gardens in front of the entrance doors'. There has been no fundamental change to the Close since, making it the only completely medieval street remaining in England.[18]

Although Bishop Ralph had bestowed an annuity of ten pounds on his newly founded college, provided by land at Congresbury and Wookey, it was very soon recognised that this was insufficient for its needs. As early as 1384 his successor, Bishop John Harewell, granted the vicarage of Kingstone, near Ilminster, to the Dean and Chapter for the use of the vicars choral on account of their poverty. The revenues from about 60 acres of land that went with it were valued at 20 marks p.a., nearly doubling the original endowment, but more than half that sum [£9 6s.8d.] was to be paid for the celebration of a daily mass at the altar of St Katherine for the souls of King Richard II and Queen Anne, Bishop John after his death and other named beneficiaries. The grant was confirmed a few months later by the Archbishop of Canterbury. Other gifts, an acre or so here, a house and garden there, not forgetting the lands in Wellesleigh noted above, from charitably minded local people gradually increased the endowments of the college over the next few decades, but never by enough to ease the financial difficulties of the vicars. The most significant gifts were those of Canon John Huish in 1361, comprising property in the High Street, which was to become the Christopher or New Inn, and of Sub-dean Nicholas Pontesbury, who bequeathed property in Southover in 1371. It is worth noting that in the late 1300s, the income of the college at York was about £160 p.a., although from this sum the college was responsible for administering a large number of the Minster's obits and chantry chapels. Land was not the only form of gift that the college received. In 1443 it could be ordered that all the jewels belonging to the Hall be put out on display and in the same year, 'one good pair of vestments of white Tarteryn with stars' was given by Thomas Bell for use only by the priest, i.e. whoever was officiating in the chapel.[19]

When Thomas Bekynton, Keeper of the Privy Seal, became bishop in 1443, he resigned his post in the royal administration and devoted most of his time, not to mention the see's annual income of about £2,000, to his episcopal duties for the next twenty-two years. When he turned his attention to the affairs of the College it was obvious that things were not well. Although he had nothing to do with the appointment of the vicars or the payment of their emoluments, he did exercise paternal authority over them. In 1445 he appointed commissioners to make an enquiry about 'the many excesses, insolences and abuses against the sacred canons, the honour of the clerical order and the statutes and ordinances of their church'. Quite what these offences were is not expanded upon and the College register is, perhaps unsurprisingly, also silent, but in 1439 the Chapter had been forced to pay the expenses of a vicar (plus servant and two horses) to travel to London to consult Bishop Stafford, Chancellor of England, 'about the arrest of the vicars during Divine service'. Nothing much seems to have been done as a result of Bekynton's commission and it was not until 1459 that he made a formal visitation and as a result he re-issued and expanded Bishop Ralph's original statutes, tightening up the organisation of the college and the general behaviour of the vicars. At the same time Bekynton issued a set of statutes for the choristers. He had been educated himself at Winchester and had been one of leading figures connected with Henry VI's foundation of Eton and it is clear from the two sets of statutes that he was more interested in the careful upbringing of the boys than the control of their elders.[20]

Until the late middle ages, the six choristers had been rather neglected. The precentor had been responsible for their musical education, such as it was, and they may have attended the grammar school under the control of the chancellor; this was mainly designed for somewhat older boys, some of them former choristers and some boys from the town. Bishop Ralph of Shrewsbury found them living with canons and treated as servants because no rents had been assigned for their food and clothing; because of their poverty they had to seek a living elsewhere, which often resulted in absence from divine offices. In 1347 he settled on them a yearly income of ten marks and built a house for them and their master, the remains of which still stand, now incorporated into the staircase up to the cathedral restaurant. Under Bishop Ralph's new regime, the choristers had a master of their own. He was appointed by the precentor from among the vicars choral, though his duties and payment do not appear to specified anywhere. Apart from singing, he gave the boys religious instruction and taught them Latin, in effect providing a choristers' school for the first time. Just over a century later, when Bishop Bekynton was drawing up his set of statutes for the choristers, he particularly commended the rules and ordinances which had recently been successfully instituted by Robert Catour, an 'excellent man of worthy memory', and used them as a basis for his own statutes. Catour was a vicar and master of the choristers as well as organist in the 1420s, and Bekynton's Rules note that Catour's ordinances had been diligently and dutifully observed in his time. By the beginning of the fifteenth century the instruction of the choristers usually included the teaching of polyphonic music.

Bishop Bekynton set out very clearly what manner of man he thought the master should be. The precentor was to look 'without any carnal affection or partiality in the matter', for a man who was a priest, and who was approved of by all for his learning and character. He was to be chaste in his own life so that he might give a stainless example of purity to the boys and more firmly correct them in the event of any impurity. He had to be knowledgeable in grammar and learned in plain song and prick song and capable of judging not only the voices of potential choristers, but their natural disposition for carrying out the office of chorister. Finally, he had to be honest and trustworthy and have enough temporal goods of his own so that he might scrupulously and faithfully dispose of the provisions and goods of the choristers. Strict rules were also laid down for the behaviour of the choristers themselves, both in the cathedral and in their house, and the bishop specified the prayers they were to say and the clothes they were to wear and even how they might amuse themselves. The Rules, however, have very little to say about their musical training. In his care for the choristers, Bekynton was again following the pattern of his predecessor, Bishop Ralph.[21]

In return for the vicars' acceptance of the re-issue of their statutes, in 1459-60 Bishop Bekynton built for them what later became known as the Chain Gate, a bridge between their hall and the cathedral at his own expense (500 marks). This enabled them to pass directly from any business they might have in the hall to their places in the quire or chapels in the dry and avoiding the traffic and pedestrians passing along the main Bath road beneath them. The staircase on the cathedral side was an extension of the stairs to the Chapter House, but its exact position entailed a small dog-leg to bring the entrance into the screens passage between the main hall and the buttery, rather than directly into the buttery. The loss of two windows because of the new work led to the insertion of a window high in the west wall because otherwise that end of the hall would have been unacceptably dark. The Dean and Chapter graciously granted the members of the college a common way from their hall down into the cathedral but the two doors inserted, one at the entrance to the steps from the cathedral and the other at the start of the bridge itself, were to be fitted with locks and the keys in the charge of the cathedral sacrist, who would open the doors at the necessary times. The vicars were also charged with the maintenance of the new way. In February 1460 the two principals and the whole fellowship of vicars choral acknowledged the great benefit they derived from the building of the Chain Gate, for which in return the bishop had asked for nothing but their prayers. They therefore pledged that every time any vicar passed along that way, either going to or coming from the cathedral he would say the *Pater Noster* and *Ave Maria* for the good estate of the bishop during his lifetime and for the soul of Bishop Ralph, and after Bekynton's death, for his soul too. In addition, after the latter event, all the vicars who were present each day at matins would gather round the tombs of Bishop Ralph and Bishop Thomas (both close together in the quire) to say the psalm *De profundis* and collects for the souls of the two bishops.[22]

Bishop Bekynton next undertook the major repair of the vicars' houses themselves, almost certainly re-roofing them all, replacing original thatch with slates and planning the strikingly tall chimney shaft extensions to each house, which were erected by his executors.[23] Last but by no means least, Bishop Bekynton's munificence to the College extended to the purchase of the small manor of Shipham in Cheddar from Lady Hungerford for £280, and in January 1468, presumably on his instructions, his executors made over the manor, comprising about 60 acres of rich pastureland, to the Dean and Chapter for the use and support of the vicars. At the time the manor had a rent roll of about £10 p.a. The bishop's will also allocated the enormous sum of £400 for the purchase of sumptuous copes for the canons and vicars of his cathedral church.[24] A year before the gift of Shipham, the vicars had also been fortunate enough to be given one third part of the manor of Newton Plecy and the advowson of the chapel there by John Kaynell and his wife Christine, part of whose inheritance it was. The sole proviso was that from the profits, John and Christine should be paid the annual sum of £5 6s.8d. during their lifetimes. A few days later, a second third part of the manor was released to them by John Pedewell, himself a vicar and the heir of John Pedewell, a recently deceased canon of the cathedral.[25] Newton Plecy, in North Petherton, comprised about 20 houses and 250 acres of pasture as rich as that at Cheddar. The financial problems of the College were by no means over, but they were substantially eased.

CHAPTER THREE
TO THE REFORMATION AND BEYOND

The period between Bishop Bekynton's generosity to the college, which was almost a re-foundation, and the Reformation was in many ways the high point of its long existence. It lasted less than a century, but during that time the vicars were adequately paid, their communal living soundly, though not generously, funded, their houses comfortable and in good repair. It is during this period of the late fifteenth century that the term 'vicars choral' came into use instead of the more general 'vicars'. In his charter Bekynton referred to them as 'perpetual vicars'. A few years after his death the record of the transfer of one third of the manor of Newton Plecy copied into the vicars' cartulary states that it was for the use of the 'vicars choral of the cathedral church'. The scribe highlighted the phrase with an asterisk in the margin, as though it were something unusual. It is used in several more documents in the cartulary, all associated with Dr Hugh Sugar, lawyer, canon and one of Bishop Bekynton's executors.[1] Whether or not he invented the term, it was an appropriate one to differentiate the singing men from other minor clergy in the cathedral at a time when developments in music in the fifteenth and early sixteenth centuries were giving depth to their professional lives. The court and the Chapel Royal, together with a handful of noblemen, employed the best professional musicians, but in general cathedrals choirs provided the main career path for most musicians and positions as organists were held by the great composers of their day.

Organs had been present in cathedrals and major churches since the Anglo-Saxon period. The first organ in the new cathedral at Wells seems from the surviving architectural evidence to have been placed on a platform high above the nave, opposite the entrance from the North Porch and to have been built in 1310, when the first written record referring to it occurs; namely that some of the timber being felled at Winscombe and earmarked for other purposes, should be used for its building. Exactly when its position was moved onto the stone screen or pulpitum at the west end of the quire is a matter for conjecture, but almost certainly soon after the pulpitum was built in about 1335. By the second half of the fourteenth century this was almost invariably its position in English cathedrals, and thus the main organ was never on the same level as the choir. Comparatively little is known about the organ's function during services and its exact place among the other elements of liturgical ceremonial. One of its main roles seems to have been to combine with small groups of soloists in the pulpitum to perform motets and parts of the Mass and which were set in polyphony, in contrast to the more customary plainsong, for important festivals. There was a second, smaller organ in the Lady Chapel at floor level. Both organs were substantially rebuilt between 1414 and 1418 and had two major overhauls as well as minor repairs in the remainder of the fifteenth century.[2]

At Wells annual payments involving the organ are first recorded in 1344, when the keeper of the organ, i.e. organist, received a salary of 13s.4d. p.a., but the first named vicar choral ' for keeping the organ and playing on it' was Walter Vagele in 1417, who received 10s. extra for the task.[2] Between 1421 and 1460, the post of organist was held by Robert Catour, who received an additional sum of 6s.8d. p.a. for 'playing the organ'. This Catour was clearly related to, possibly the nephew of, the man whose rules for the choristers had so impressed Bishop Bekynton that he felt he could do no better than reiterate them. The younger Catour is first recorded as a vicar in 1421, when he was paid as organist, but by 1461-2 he was sharing the organist's stipend with four other vicars, which suggests that he may have been unwell or possibly absent from Wells. In other cathedrals and churches the duty of organist was discharged by a team drawn from the vicars, and in sometimes having a single organist, Wells was comparatively unusual.

Catour was still active in 1469, when he was vicar principal, and seems to have died in the later part of that year. He was succeeded as organist by John Menyman, who was that rare creature, a vicar choral who eventually became a canon. He entered the college as a probationer in 1451 and it would seem that his quality was soon recognised, because in 1454 he was granted leave of absence for three years to proceed to the schools of Oxford. Such licences were given on standard terms and were granted throughout the centuries, though they were more usually for a year for vicars to travel to Rome. The absent vicar gave up 'all profits, commons and emoluments belonging to a perpetual vicar, apart from 26s.8d. yearly from his vicar's stall, meeting the cost in the meanwhile of an incumbency for the said stall'. In other words, the vicar had to have a generous patron or some other means of support during his absence because his income in Wells went towards paying a substitute. At the end of the three years, Menyman returned to Wells, where he became joint organist briefly in 1461-2 and then held the post permanently between 1470 and 1491. In addition he served the Chapter diligently in a variety of posts, including that of communar (the chief financial officer) on a number of occasions. He was rewarded with the perpetual vicarage of St Cuthbert's in 1488 and finally, in

1493, was granted the prebend of Dinder and became a canon residentiary.[3]

Plainsong had been an integral part of the Christian liturgy since its earliest days, but in the later middle ages, polyphony entered the liturgy because of its ability to add ceremonial distinction to the more important parts and mark out major services from the lesser without changing the ritual text or music. The masses of the day might be sung with relative simplicity on weekdays; the series of services ran from daybreak for most of the morning, the two most important being the Lady Mass at about 9.00am and the high mass an hour later. On Sundays and feast days they were celebrated with magnificence. Polyphony might alternate with plainsong or replace it altogether in the ordinary of the mass (Gloria, Credo, Sanctus, Benedictus and Agnus Dei), and antiphons or motets appropriate to the liturgical season could be included. The Marian masses sung in the Lady Chapel provided the greatest opportunity for the performance of elaborate polyphonic music sung by trained voices. Vespers, the last service of the day, where the liturgy contained the Magnificat, was one also of the most important services musically by the late 15th century.

Thus, by the second half of the fifteenth century English church music had been transformed. New compositions included full choruses instead of teams of soloists, and boys' voices were used for the first time in composed polyphonic music. The number of vicars had been gradually reducing (because of a similar reduction in the number of canons) since the high point of about fifty; in 1437 there were 34 vicars and by 1500 about two dozen. For the same period there were six boy choristers at Wells, a surprisingly low number: Salisbury and Exeter had fourteen choristers and York had twelve. Choristers served for about four or five years on average and when their voices broke they were usually sent to the grammar school with a stipend, and if particularly clever might be funded through university. Those who continued to be interested in music and had a good adult voice might become vicars, as did Robert White in 1488, but not until they were 22 years old and thus eligible to be accepted into minor orders. Any man appointed as master of the choristers had to be a skilled and trained musician, not only able to teach the boys their parts in polyphonic compositions, but also creating those compositions as the cathedral services demanded. Richard Hygons was the first man known to have combined the role of organist with that of master of the choristers, but he is important for more than that. His contract for the post of master in 1479 is the only surviving one of its kind and contains a full description of his duties. Not that he would have been unfamiliar with them because he had already been a vicar choral for 20 years.[4]

Hygons was contracted to instruct the choristers in plainsong and in improvised and composed polyphony and to teach the organ to those who had the talent to learn. He was also to sing at the daily Lady Mass in the Lady Chapel and at the customary singing of the antiphon in honour of the Virgin at her image situated at the north side of the entrance to the quire. Immediately after that on Sundays he was to direct the choristers in singing the Jesus-antiphon before the great cross in the nave. Some of the music Hygons composed is still extant, including two elaborate settings of the Mary antiphon. In 1497 he received a gratuity of ten shillings on the orders of the dean 'for certain matters in preparation for the Feast of Easter', which may well have been for a specific composition. There is evidence of the success of the Wells choristers under his tutelage when two of the boys, in 1493 and 1505, were taken away for service in the king's Chapel Royal. On the first occasion the Chapter paid both the king's servants and the queen's players not to take away their three best choristers and were lucky to have got away with losing only one. In recognition of all his skills, Hygons was very well paid. In 1487 'for his diligence and good service' he was granted for life as an augmentation of his salary the sum of 26s.8d. issuing from a vacant stall. In total he received a stipend of £4 13s.4d. and a house valued at 26s.8d. (the Choristers' House). He finally added the duty of organist to those of master of the choristers, probably in 1493 when the then organist, John Menyman resigned on becoming a canon. He held both posts until 1507 and probably died the following year; the two posts have usually, but not invariably, been combined ever since.[5]

Hygons' successor as master of the choristers and organist was Richard Bramston, the last of a trio of distinguished men who held that position at Wells in the late 15th and early 16th centuries. He was admitted as a probationer vicar choral in January 1507 and within six months the Chapter agreed that Hygons should pay Bramston 40s. per year for deputising for him in teaching the choristers to sing 'as Hygons did in times past', and playing the organs in the Quire and Lady Chapel. Clearly he was already recognised as a talented musician, but unfortunately he was less satisfactory as a person. When the time came for him to be perpetuated, this did not go through on the nod; he was perpetuated on the condition that he was diligent in reading, singing plainsong and learning the psalter in the following year. A few months later, in May1508, his position as Hygons' deputy was removed by the formal appointment of John Clawsy as Hygons' successor as master and organist, although the aged Hygons retained a proportion of the salary as a pension. Finally in September 1509, Bramston was warned that he must take sub-deacon's orders by Christmas on pain of deprivation. It seems that he preferred to leave Wells and take up the post of master of the Lady Chapel choir at St Augustine's Abbey, Bristol (now Bristol Cathedral).

Bramston's next connection with Wells comes in a furious letter written in February 1510 by the Chapter to the absent dean describing how Bramston had come in 'privy and [disguised] apparel, to have hadde away one of our best queresters, that is to say, Farre' and taken him to Bristol to augment the choir there. The Chapter then asked contacts in London to obtain from the king a protection to stop it happening again and at the same time have his favour for them to take any child from a monastery or elsewhere in the diocese to serve St Andrew. Subsequently, Bramston mended fences and returned to Wells as a vicar in about 1515 and was re-instated as master of the choristers and probably also as organist, this time with no requirement for ordination. The situation in the previous few years seems to have been somewhat unsatisfactory, with various of the vicars filling in as master of the choristers or as organist; for instance in 1512 one of the vicars, John Gye, was given 26s.8d. as a reward for his diligent instruction of the choristers. The Chapter were therefore presumably influenced in favour of Bramston's return. Two of Bramston's compositions – Latin antiphons – survive and he seems to have had a considerable reputation as a composer among his contemporaries. He served several times as keeper of the fabric for the Chapter, the last time in 1549-50, and on his death in 1554 his will showed that he had become prosperous and left much of his wealth for charitable purposes. This included three small houses in Tor Lane to the Dean and Chapter for the benefit of the Fabric Fund. For how long Bramston served as master of the choristers after his re-instatement is unclear, but in 1538 John Smith was collated to the chantry in the chapel of All Saints in the Palm churchyard as a reward 'for his diligence in instructing the choristers and for his great pains in composing a number of pieces of music for the augmentation of divine worship'. From the proceeds he was to provide himself with 'square books and pricke songe books' for the choir, for the Lady Chapel and the processions on the principal feasts and leave them to his successors. The grant was for life, but the chantry was paid for by the Hospital of St Mark, Bristol, and if the revenues from this source failed, the Chapter would not compensate him.[6] Smith had been serving as organist in place of Bramston from at least 1534 but unfortunately no music by him is known to have survived and the books he provided were lost, along with most of the cathedral's medieval music, at the Reformation.

There are relatively few references to the vicars' performance of their duties in church in the records of either college or Chapter. One case the Chapter did deal with was that of vicar William Baron, who on 1 December 1490 was condemned because although he had the rule of the choir on the feast of St. Andrew, he had neglected to do that office for matins, either in person or by arranging a substitute. The scandal and 'evil example' to other vicars was all the greater because it was the patronal festival. He was suspended from wearing his habit or receiving any commons for a month. In 1578 a vicar was admonished for leaving the cathedral during service time and repairing to St Cuthbert's, and was reminded he must give his attendance and service to the cathedral. The vicars took seriously their right to veto new appointments, either before a singer joined them or at the end of their probationary year. In 1507 fifteen named vicars testified in Chapter that probationer Gilbert Frances had not a competent voice and was of evil conversation, and the precentor, with the consent of Chapter, decreed that he should not be perpetuated.

The communal life of the College during the late fifteenth and early sixteenth centuries proceeded smoothly save for a few minor hiccups. Some of its members cared little for its governance and were quite happy to give voice to their dissent. In 1521 Henry Paston spoke out against the statutes 'wickedly and contrary to good manners', and did so in the presence of his fellows at dinner, compounding the offence by calling Hugh Vesey a drunken knave and a liar. Deprived of all common dues relating to the hall, it only took him four days to back down and apologise. Absence from hall meetings without good reason was frowned upon and usually led to deprivation of commons, although repentence or an appeal usually led to reinstatement: in 1533 John Braddon, who had been deprived, pleaded his bodily infirmity and John Smith, one of the principals that year, decreed he should be restored.[7] The position of vicars who could no longer perform their duties satisfactorily was a vexed one. Their posts were for life, and it would certainly have been unchristian to have dismissed them; what seems to have happened is that they remained in post, receiving their dues and payments, but from them provided a substitute who received considerably less that perpetuated vicars. It was an issue which continued to cause tensions between college and Chapter until well into the twentieth century.

There is no doubt that some of the vicars came from affluent families, and one of the most generous was Richard Pomeroy. He entered the college at some point in the 1480s and swiftly became one of those vicars who were of immense use to the Chapter, serving frequently as escheator and keeper of the fabric until his death in 1523. He is best remembered, however, for the changes to the hall, which he funded. Three of the original windows are still in situ, with some medieval glass remaining in the traceries. Pomeroy was responsible for the two oriel windows on either side of the eastern end. He is depicted in the tracery on the north side as the donor, dressed in blue, requesting *'Orate pro me'*, and the arms of St Andrew encompassed with his name are in the south-east corner of the east wall. He was probably also responsible for the plainer oriel window at the western or service end of the north wall, where a shield of the Sacred Passion is surmounted by the letters POM and he may even have constructed the present plastered, barrel-vaulted ceiling; this consists of nine and a half bays with plain chamfered ribs. Within this structure, on either side of the door on the north, there are still traces of where the screens were originally fixed, marking a passage between the hall and the buttery. He is also commemorated in a Latin inscription on the mantel-shelf of the Tudor fireplace, which again asks future generations of vicars to pray for his soul. The fireplace, rebuilt from an earlier one, incorporates a pulpit high in the window embrasure, where, according to Bishop Bekynton's statutes, one of vicars was to read from the bible to his brethren during mealtimes. Medieval oak panelling survives on parts of the north and south walls, while the east wall has linen-fold panelling, not seen in England before the reign of Henry VIII, and which may also date from this major refurbishment. Apart from the removal of the screens passage, the hall as we see it now is substantially unchanged from the the early 16th century.[8]

The Reformation, when it reached England, came in several phases. The first, Henry VIII's break with Rome and the dissolution of the monasteries, had surprisingly little effect on Wells, although Bath Abbey (the only cathedral building erected chiefly in the Tudor period) surrendered in 1539 and became the principal parish church of the town. Henry did not single out secular cathedrals, and since he made no major changes in the liturgy, cathedral services continued virtually unchanged. As with all clergy, the canons had to accept the extinguishing of papal authority in England and swear to acknowledge Henry as supreme head of the church in England. In fact, they went a step further: the Dean and Chapter asking the king to give them new statutes in 1536 because they believed that their previous constitution was invalidated by the break with Rome. The government did not seem to agree and their request was ignored. A year later, the king's chief minister, Thomas Cromwell, became dean of Wells, the first layman to hold the post. It is not clear whether he actually ever visited Wells, but his influence was strongly felt as the canons surrendered to the royal authorities all the cathedral treasures which could be remotely described as Romish and for good measure the entire contents of their library as well. Wells had always regarded the fact that it did not have a saint's shrine as a serious drawback to the attraction of pilgrims and the raising of funds, but this proved to be lucky in the 1530s, since there was thus nothing to ransack. The shrine of St Richard at Chichester – not one of the major ones – produced a ship's coffer full of gold, silver and jewels for the king's commissioners to confiscate. It made little practical difference to the Wells canons that after 1534 their clerical annates (the entire first year's profits from Church offices and ten per cent p.a. thereafter) were paid to the Crown rather than to Rome, but the *Valor Ecclesiasticus,* compiled a year later, updated the valuations, so as a result they paid more to the Crown than they had ever done to the pope.[9]

The blow from which Wells and its vicars really suffered came in 1547 with the abolition of chantries. The exact number of these at Wells has not been conclusively calculated, but in that year, 77 obits were celebrated and there seem to have been nineteen chantries, most served by annuellers or chantry priests, although Bishop Beckington's chantry and that of Dean Gunthorpe in the Lady Chapel were served only by canons, and others, including the Bitton chantry at the altar of St Nicholas in the Lady Chapel in the Cloister and Cookham's chantry in All Saints Chapel in the Palm Churchyard were served by vicars choral who were priests. The fourteen chantry chaplains had been provided with their own hall, Monterey, by Bishop Ralph Erghum in 1399. At a stroke, all this vanished, the income from the endowments supporting the chantries at the wish of their donors becoming reserved to the crown. It was not just the payments to the chantry priests which vanished; at each of the benefactors' anniversary services, known as obits, a payment was distributed among all the clergy and vicars who attended and since the number of obits was many, the cash payments made a significant contribution to each vicar's income. All this was now diligently collected by the king's receiver each year: for the year 1550/1 Master John Aylworthe received well over a hundred pounds from the Chapter in total; the proportion due to the Crown from obits was assessed at £48 1s. 4d., much of which would previously have gone to priest vicars or other chantry chaplains. From henceforth, after he had paid the crown dues, the escheator divided the balance of about £20 equally among canons, vicars and choristers. While much of the money earmarked for the obits and anniversaries was paid to the Crown, the lands which provided a large proportion of this income remained in the hands of the Chapter who leased them and thus benefited from all increases in rents and fines on grants of new leases. The Chapter then divided any surplus among themselves, without necessarily paying any share of it to the vicars and choristers. After the abolition of chantries, the vicars who had served as chantry priests were to some extent protected by their singing role, but the other chaplains could not be cast out upon the street, and the Chapter had to find other roles and payments for them somehow until over time they dispersed and found other employment. The number of vicars at this period fell to about ten.[10]

While the liturgy altered little under Henry VIII, the accession of his son Edward VI, head of an ardently Protestant government, led almost immediately to changes. A letter from the king's commissioners dated 1 November 1547 forbade the wearing of vestments and the tolling of funeral bells. It also referred specifically to the priest vicars, ordering one of them to read in the Quire, immediately after high mass on holy days, one of the homilies in a book the king had ordered printed for the instruction of his people. A month later, the time of this reading was ordered to be moved from the afternoon to the morning, immediately before high mass, and the service of prime was to be omitted to accommodate it. This was the beginning of great changes to the liturgy. In 1549 Parliament authorised the first English Prayer Book. The Roman mass and the daily cycle of offices, which had required the constant attendance of the vicars in the cathedral, was replaced by just three main services, Matins, Holy Communion and Evensong, and Holy Communion was celebrated only once or twice a month. In addition, all the services had now to be conducted in English and this meant a considerable expenditure on behalf of the Chapter to provide the new service books. There was thus a substantial reduction in the amount of singing required of the vicars and this dramatic change in their professional lives was paralleled by the approval, granted by Convocation in the same year, of clergy marriage. While many of them had found celibacy difficult, supporting a wife and family on a vicar's income proved even more of a challenge. It is from the mid 16th century, therefore, that the pattern of the vicars' lives took on the shape familiar to vicars today as they sought part-time employment. Sometimes this was working for the Chapter itself as master of the fabric, communar, or escheator, which meant that much of the financial management of the cathedral was in the hands of vicars, keeping the college closely tied to the affairs of the Chapter. For many vicars, employment took the form of teaching, but any other work for which an individual was competent was accepted. They had to be present for the services, but the Chapter had no interest in how they spent the rest of their time, provided that they did nothing that brought the cathedral into disrepute.

The life of the college may have been turned upside down in the 1540s, but one constant was the business of running their estates. Henry VIII's *Valor Ecclesiasticus* provides the first overall survey of their landed property. At Wells, the survey records, the total pre-Reformation income of the vicars was £208 11s. 2d. p.a., very similar to those of Salisbury and Exeter; the difference was that in the latter two cases, the income was shared by about 20 vicars, while at Wells the number, once as high as 50, had sunk to 23 in 1500 and by the 1540s was only 10, giving each vicar an income of approximately £20 p.a., higher than it was to be for many years to come. Of the total, £72 10s. 9d. came from rents.[11] Much the largest sum, £20, came from the church and land at Kingstone, while the estates at Newton Plecy, Cheddar and Martock brought in between £6-9 each and the urban property in Wells about £10. The Wells properties made the vicars the fourth largest institutional landlord in the town after the corporation, the Dean and Chapter and the trustees of Bubwith's Almshouses. Their holdings were scattered throughout the town, though with small concentrations in Chamberlain Street and Southover. In a number of cases the properties were not held directly by the College but were granted to a group of vicars, the last survivors of whom granted it on to a further group. By this means there had been no need to pay for a license in mortmain [a crown charge on property to be held by institutions in lieu of feudal dues] and gave the vicars concerned a degree of independence; most of the properties had been granted by fellow clergy to fund obits for themselves. The single most valuable Wells property was that known as the New Inn or the Christopher on the High Street, at the corner with Howsel Lane. It was given to the vicars in perpetuity by Canon John Huish in the mid fourteenth century in return for a rent of 13d. pa. and 8s. pa. as an obit for his soul. In the early 1420s the landlord, John Whyte, was paying a rent of £4 13s. 4d. pa. for the inn.

The remainder of the vicars' rents came from scattered holdings outside the town. This, at least, was the theory. In practice rent arrears were substantial, often the equivalent of two years' total income. It was the responsibility of the manor steward or reeve to collect the rents, but it was often left to the college principals to ride out and bring back the rents to Wells to the hands of their receiver. The serious disadvantage of this system was that there was no continuity of administration at the college. Each pair of principals and each receiver was concerned only with the outcome of their own year of office and nobody was responsible for planning or forward thinking, let alone keeping the stewards and reeves on their toes or ensuring that arrears of rent were paid. A further cause of failure was that any vicar who appeared to have a talent for administration was appointed by the Chapter to its own paid posts, posts that they often filled for years, rather than annually like the college offices. The lack of business acumen thus available to the college almost certainly meant that the vicars received considerably less each year from their estates than they should have done. This did not prevent them in 1541 from appointing a clerk, John Smith, notary public, to record 'all and singular the acts and business of the New Close', for which he received the sum of 6s.8d. p.a. as remuneration. The Act book that Smyth began dutifully records the entry of each new vicar, leases granted and the occasional disciplinary matter. He also notes in 1551 that the weekly charge of 6d. that each vicar paid for his commons in hall was to double 'to support and relieve the heavy burden on this place' and that the cup of wine both at dinner and supper was to be discontinued. In 1552 Bishop William Barlow made a visitation of the college, decreeing that all men guilty of quarrels in the New Close should be expelled and deprived of all commons and profits. There are also tantalisingly damaged entries which appear to refer to the wives of vicars.[12]

In 1551 the Protestant government of Edward VI appointed William Turner as dean, but although a reformer, he was not a fanatic, and many of the Chapter had been in office for years. One consequence of his reforms was that the responsibilities of the various officers of the Chapter increased and were undertaken by the residentiary canons, so that the vicars lost the posts such as communar and master of the fabric that they had frequently held in the past. Only the escheatorship remained and the Chapter selected one of two nominated vicars to serve for a year. Since the obits and anniversaries were Romish practices no longer observed, the escheator simply had to divide the surplus in fixed proportions among the canons and vicars after the Crown had received its dues. Over the ensuing decades the two groups, canons and vicars, grew slowly much less close than they had been in the pre-Reformation period.

Under the new regime, music itself does not seem to have suffered. In about 1550 William Parsons came to the cathedral, almost certainly as organist, though there is no specific reference to him as such. He was a composer of some note and there are a number of specific additional payments made to him by order of Chapter for 'certain canticles and books by him made and to be made'. None of his compositions, however, remain at Wells. In October 1557 Robert Awman was appointed as organist and master of the choristers at a salary of £12 p.a., but if Parsons was replaced as organist, the Chapter was still commissioning canticles from him in 1558. Most sets of choir part-books were compiled by the vicars themselves. William Lyde, both organist and master of the grammar school, purchased eight quires of paper in 1561 'to make books into which the same songs and others could be pricked'; he had also purchased 'a good song, viz. Te Deum in English' on a visit to Hereford. Likewise, Alexander Ward was also paid for songs which he brought from Gloucester and Bristol; clearly the vicars were all encouraged to keep their ears open for new music they heard elsewhere, slowly enlarging their repertoire in English.[13]

The brief Marian reaction [1553-1558] saw the restoration of the mass and use of Latin as well as other forms of traditional worship which may have been welcomed by the majority of the clerical establishment at Wells. We know nothing of the theological beliefs of the vicars and only one of the canons, the Chancellor, John Cardmaker alias Taylor, a former friar who had married, was burned at Smithfield as a martyr, though since he was also a Divinity reader at St Paul's, it may have been his London activities which brought him to the stake. At Wells there was a rapid refurbishment of the altars, long since stripped of all embellishment save for two candlesticks, and lavish expenditure on new copes, tunics and dalmatics in the cathedral. In 1555, with the consent of all the vicars, it was decreed that four times a year, obsequies should be solemnly celebrated for the founders and all the benefactors of the college. On 15 October 1556 the New Close chapel was reconsecrated by the new suffragan bishop of Taunton, William Fynche, in honour of St Andrew the Apostle. It was noted that the chapel had been 'dishonoured and profaned by the most wicked enemies of Christ and worst heretics'; whether this referred to strongly Protestant vicars or outsiders is not indicated. Why the dedication was changed is also unknown. The former one, in honour of the Assumption and St Katherine was impeccably Catholic, but in the changing times that were to come, St Andrew, to whom the cathedral itself was dedicated, proved more acceptable. Probably the least welcome of the Marian changes would have been the return of celibacy. It is not clear whether any married canons or vicars were deprived at Wells, or whether wives discreetly disappeared to accommodation elsewhere.[14]

On the accession of Elizabeth in 1558 the pendulum swung halfway back. As the Supreme Governor (not 'Head' as her father had been) of the Church in England, she restored what had existed earlier but had been interrupted by her sister Mary. While devoutly Protestant, she was not an innovator like her brother Edward, but more inclined to return things to their position at the end of her father's reign. Nevertheless Edward's English Prayer Book was restored and a series of injunctions in 1559 had a number of practical repercussions for cathedrals in particular. Processions were to be abandoned, but the litany was retained and was to be said or sung in churches at the beginning of the communion service. The queen herself opposed clerical marriage, but her wise minister, William Cecil, knew that the government would have to rely on priests who had married under Edward, so all Elizabeth could do was to impose obstacles. Initially there was nothing she could do about clergy who were already married, but those intending to marry from henceforth had to have their future wife examined and approved by the bishop of their diocese. Two years later, however, the wives and families of canons and other members of cathedrals and colleges were forbidden to live within the precincts because their presence violated the intention of the founders and were a distraction to study and learning. The enforcement of this ruling was the responsibility of the bishop, who dealt with it according to his own views on the matter; luckily most did not enforce this too strictly. By this stage, one or two of the houses in the Close may have already been joined together in pairs to provide larger houses for married vicars.[15]

Fortunately for the vicars of Wells and elsewhere, Elizabeth loved music. She had no wish for the tradition of men and boys singing to the glory of God to come to an end – unlike the more extreme Protestants who wanted such distractions done away with. To appease them, an injunction was issued that the new services in English were to be sung modestly and distinctly so that all the words could be heard and understood 'as if it were read without singing', while at the end of morning and evening prayer a more elaborate hymn or song was permitted 'in the best sort of melody and music that may be conveniently devised'. The result was the great flowering of Elizabethan church music under the likes of Tallis and Byrd, although at Wells the greatest period of creativity seems to have been the earlier Tudor period. There is very little information on the repertoire performed at Wells in the later 16th century, nothing listing the anthems and services as they were sung day by day, and there are no recorded comments from those who heard them. As well as music, the queen was known to enjoy theatrical performances by the 'Children of Powles', that is, choristers and other pupils at St Paul's School, who with the encouragement of Dean Colet, produced dramas. The only other evidence of similar plays put on by other cathedrals comes from Wells. In 1583 the headmaster of the grammar school was admonished for taking his students, including choristers, to Axbridge, to play in the parish church. It is not clear what the objection was. The Chapter may simply have disapproved of plays performed in churches, or of the children travelling round the diocese, but the master was fined two shillings – one penny for each of the two dozen inmates of the almshouse, who presumably received the benefit of the fine.

As things settled down under Elizabeth, the vicars recruited as many as seven new members in the autumn of 1562. One of them was a man called John Weekes, whom a year later the college unanimously refused to perpetuate. Weekes apparently had friends in high places because in December 1563, the principals received a letter from Richard Edwardes, master of the choristers at the Chapel Royal, asking them to reconsider and if they agree 'I shall cause my betters to give you all thanckes. And yf anie of youe need there ffriendshippe in the courte, to have it redy as a thinge dewe for this good turne'. The principals replied firmly but fulsomely that the statutes of both the college and cathedral did not admit such reconsideration and that Weekes had been refused for perpetuation because he was old and his voice decaying. They explained somewhat plaintively that their number already included certain vicars who had served for many years and while they could no longer serve they had still to be supported, so that all new recruits needed to 'bringe youthe and good qualities wid them'. They also pointed out they understood Weekes 'is otherwise well provided to lyve and a gentle man borne in his contry'. This does rather beg the question of why he was admitted as a probationer in the first place; perhaps the number of vicars was so depleted they were willing to take all who applied, or perhaps sickness had aged him considerable within that year. Perhaps things had changed by 1579, when John Gibson, one of the vicars, was charged with taking a bribe of 10s. from Robert Trycer for his goodwill in his admission to the college. Gibson admitted that he did so but refused to refund the money and appealed to the bishop. Trycer's case seems an odd one; he was admitted as a probationer in October 1575, but there is no further record of him until he is admitted a probationer once again in March 1579, a month before Gilbert was charged. Again there is no further reference to him. Gibson, however, was in further trouble a few months later for uttering 'opprobious and threatening words against the sub-dean, Philip Bisse, and suffered the loss of his matins money for a month and had to come before the Chapter and humbly upon his knees confess his fault and ask forgiveness of Mr Bisse. His record did not prevent him from going on to serve as one of the college principals.[16]

There were occasions when the vicars of Wells had reasons to rue the queen's love of music. In about 1583 one of the Wells choristers, a boy named John Pitcher, was recruited to the Chapel Royal. Pitcher sang in the choir there for about six years until his voice broke. The dean, Valentine Dale (one of a trio of Elizabethan lawyers who were made lay deans and who rarely visited Wells), wrote on the queen's behalf to the Chapter requesting that the young man be made a vicar choral, there being a current vacancy. For whatever reason the Chapter did not do as it was asked; perhaps this was another occasion when the college refused to agree to an appointment on musical grounds. The result was a letter signed personally by Elizabeth on 15 March 1589 in which her secretary sets out her request, pointing out that the boy 'hath remained nighe this sixe yeares…in our chaple ….diligent in service and to our goode likinge, till nowe, that his voice begynneth to chaunge, hee is become not soe fitt for our service', and that with the vacancy in the ranks of the vicars choral of Wells, he should be appointed to fill it. It was a perfect opportunity for the queen to reward her former chorister with a position at no cost to herself. Her letter was accompanied by one containing a stinging rebuke from the dean that the queen had been 'made to have written her selfe in soe smalle a matter'. Despite this, John Pitcher did not become a member of the college, though why we do not know; probably some other patron made him a better offer.

How did the queen know that there was a vacancy for a vicar at Wells? Because only a few months before, in January 1589, a vicar named John Hulett sought permission to reside at court pursuant to an appointment made by the queen's council; unfortunately no mention is made of what that appointment was, but it was almost certainly for his singing voice because the Chapter offered him an additional forty shillings a year to remain at Wells or if he was determined to go to court, they would continue to pay him provided that when he was not attendant on the queen, he spent the rest of his time at the cathedral. There is no record of which choice Hulett made, though he certainly continued as a vicar. The generosity of the Chapter's offer suggests that he had an exceptional voice, particularly because a year before, when he was serving as Principal, he was warned 'That from henceforth he doe better and more diligentlie use and exercise his office in the quier accordinge to the laudable Use and Custome of the church'. Perhaps he had been absent from his duties pursuing his career at court.[17]

None of the men who followed William Lyde as organist from 1562 seem to have made much of a mark. John Clerke, appointed in 1587, was never master of the choristers but held office in the cathedral as escheator and tabellar for varying periods; he was described as one of the principal vicars rather than organist when he was deprived of one quarter's emoluments in 1606 for refusing to admit into the college a probationary vicar called John Fido, who had been chosen by the Dean and Chapter. The usual reason for such refusal was that the candidate did not pass the vicars' test of competent singing. Fido may not have been much of a singer, but he is described elsewhere as 'a man very skilfull in ye arte of musick' and held an appointment as an organist elsewhere. There are no further details of the disagreement between Clerke and the Chapter, but also no other references to Fido anywhere in the records of either Chapter or college, so it seems likely that the vicars' right to veto the appointment to their college stood. The displeasure of the Chapter is clear because as well as depriving Clerke of emoluments it ordered him to enter deacon's orders within a year. After the Reformation this requirement, though still on the statute books, had been quietly dropped. Some vicars, of course, chose to become priests but with the abolition of chantries there was less need for priests, and many, perhaps most, vicars remained simply lay musicians.[18]

At Wells the number of vicars choral rose from a low point of ten and for most of Elizabeth's reign stabilised at between 15 and 17, similar to York and slightly lower than St Paul's and Exeter, though it sometimes rose as high as 24. Everywhere vicars choral suffered from financial distress. Their resources failed to keep pace with inflation and some now had to provide for wives and families as well (see Appendix 3). The College Act book meticulously records the entry of each new vicar for his probationary year, four in 1566, two more the following year. In 1575 there was discussion over the perpetuation of Thomas Fisher as a vicar. Three members of Chapter refused to agree to it, while the three others were firmly in favour and in the end the perpetuation went ahead despite the fact that the majority of the vicars had pronounced him musically incompetent; in this case, therefore, their veto failed to take effect. Nor were these the only disputes over the appointment of vicars. In 1579 John Taylor was expelled as a vicar by the Dean and Chapter because he broke his oath to the college for disobeying the Chapter, refusing to admit and install Richard Evans as a vicar, even though he had already been admitted by the Chapter. This, too, was almost certainly a disagreement over musical competency and indicates that the vicars were not always able to get their own way over the use of their veto. The year of 1579, however, also saw the installation of two men who became noteworthy musicians. One was Elway Bevin, whose subsequent career took him to Bristol as master of the choristers and thence to the Chapel Royal, but not before he had been suspended in 1581 for not having received communion in four years. His settings for morning and evening services are preserved in the later part-books of the cathedral. The other late Tudor composer of note was Matthew Jefferies, who remained at Wells as master of the choristers and became one of the more important minor provincial composers whose work has survived and which 'certainly deserves an occasional hearing'. Neither of these men, however, held the post of organist.[20]

      Entries in the Act book note the fines levied by the vicars on their fellows for quarrelling and discord. Prior to the Reformation a great many of the disciplinary actions taken against vicars were for sexual offences; one Salisbury vicar charged with maintaining a concubine alleged every vicar kept a mistress and while this may not have been strictly true either at Salisbury or Wells, there were plenty of examples. In 1493 Simon Lane, not only a vicar but a chantry priest, admitted that he had committed adultery with the daughter of a local burgess and as a penance was required to go before the procession in the cathedral on the following Sunday with a wax taper he was to offer at the image of St Andrew and he was suspended from wearing his habit or receiving his pay for six months. This was a particularly harsh punishment and may have been as a result of a complaint from her father. John Harman, charged with an adulterous relationship with Joan Plummer in 1509, was given the penance of saying part of the psalter while kneeling before the image of St Andrew. The following year he was excommunicated for a few days when he admitted having a child by a woman named Maud. The ability to marry improved matters somewhat, but in 1593 Thomas Everett was charged with getting his maidservant, Joan Teight, with child and was excommunicated, while in 1600, William Tawswell was accused of incontinence with the wife of one of his colleagues, though the case was not proved. Tawswell had friends in high places, because none other than Sir Walter Raleigh wrote to the sub-dean, James Bisse, in September 1590 asking for Tawswell, a probationer, to be perpetuated. In October 1591 Tawswell resigned his place and then immediately changed his mind and asked to be re-instated. In May1592 he humbly begged again to be re-instated and after long discussion mainly because he had never been perpetuated, the Chapter finally agreed to his perpetuation. Apart from the charge of incontinence in 1600, a year later, in April 1601, he and another vicar were suspended for a month after admitting to being out all night in the town, playing at 'tables' (a form of backgammon). At some unknown date he was discharged from his position, but in a petition to the Dean and Chapter, he apologised for his 'unworthy demeanour', before going on to inform them that learned counsel (paid for by whom? Raleigh?) had said the discharge was more than the Chapter could lawfully do. He begged forgiveness and re-instatement because without his position he faced utter ruin and besides he had many children to support.[21] Disagreements between vicars or between a vicar and the college were rarely very serious and were dealt with by fines and penances and occasional excommunication. Only very rarely does evidence that any vicar was involved in more serious crime come to light. However, in the City of Wells Convocation Book on 28 February 1569, it is ordered

'that wheras Robart Everat late one of the vicar choralles of the close in Wells aforesayde hath Receyved Judgment to be hanged in Chaynes by the Justices of Assases of this counte of Somerset & therupon sent over to this Town aforesayd to be put to execucion here for that the fact wherof he is convicted was here committed, it is therfore ordred as aforesayde that Chaynes shalbe made for that purpose, and that the constables & other officers within this Towne which are bound to serve the Quene shall attende the same execucion which shalbe done the 2 of Marche after the daye aforsayde & that the sayde constables & other officers aforesayde shall not fayle theyre attendance'.

It is particularly unfortunate that the Assize records for Somerset for this period do not survive, so there is no means of knowing what Everat's crime was. To be hung in chains, rather than simply hung suggests a particularly heinous crime, almost certainly murder of some aggravated sort. Several members of the Everett or Everard family were employed in the cathedral in Elizabeth's reign, usually as virgers. Thomas Everett, noted above for incontinence, who was a vicar from 1589 until his dismissal in 1594, was probably a relative, but Robert was still only a probationer and had not been perpetuated at the time he committed his crime.[22]

Most misdemeanours were dealt with by the college, but occasionally either the Dean and Chapter or the bishop became involved. In June 1573, 'considering all the outrages, troubles, slanders, perjuries and other annoyances contrived by Dom Thomas Rumsey, contrary to the ordinances and Statutes of this place' and the injunctions of the bishop, Gilbert Berkeley, the majority of the college voted to expel Rumsay. The fact that Rumsey had some supporters suggests that the issue was not entirely clear cut. He had been admitted as a vicar in 1566 and served in several of the college offices as a senior, but in February 1570 was disciplined for having been involved in a serious disagreement of some sort with Matthew Nailer, which led to 'wrangles, disputes and quarrels'. After a reprimand, both men were fined, Nailer three times more heavily than Rumsey. There is a possible explanation for Rumsey's troubles. In 1573, John Bridgewater, prebendary of Compton Bishop, was deprived of his benefice for recusancy and fled to Douai, taking with him several students from Oxford and one of the Wells vicars choral. This was very probably Rumsey, and the disputes for which he was expelled on the instructions of the bishop, religious ones. No other vicar who could be identified as the anonymous one seems to have left in 1573 [23]

Misdemeanours dealt with by the Chapter usually involved the vicars' behaviour outside college, and it usually had recourse to depriving the erring vicar of his commons until he recanted his bad behaviour. In 1574 Chapter decreed that if any vicar visited the town and there frequented illicit games, namely the tennis court and other suchlike places, for the first offence he would be deprived of his commons for a week, for a second offence, two weeks; for a third offence a month and if he transgressed further he would be expelled if the Chapter so decided 'because as a result of vicars frequenting illicit sports, the church gets a bad name'. Puritan zeal had not succeeded in banishing music from services as they wished, but in other ways their influence was felt. They vehemently believed that preaching was of much greater significance than communion and so more frequent sermons and infrequent communion became the norm. In 1571 the queen's visitor at Wells required one of the residentiary canons to celebrate communion on the first Sunday of the month and all canons and vicars to partake. Despite this injunction, laxity prevailed. In 1581 two vicars were suspended because they had not received communion in four years and in 1596 the whole college was exhorted to receive it at least three times a year. While this does not seem too onerous, in 1599 two vicars were threatened with expulsion if they did not comply.[24]

By the second half of Elizabeth's reign, relations between college and Chapter seem to have become seriously strained. While the major issue seems to have been the regular taking of communion, in other ways too, the vicars felt that the Chapter was trying to increase its control over the college with its depleted numbers and reduced role. In the end, they took the drastic, and no doubt expensive, step of petitioning the Queen for confirmation of their rights and privileges as set out in their two previous charters. A further reason for doing so was the position of the college as a legal entity in relation to its estates; had this been altered by the changes at the Reformation? Probably not, but it was thought as well to be safe. The petition, dated 26 June 1590, was addressed to the Attorney General and Solicitor to Her Majesty.[25] At the same time and for many of the same reasons, the Dean and Chapter were presenting their own petition for a new charter to confirm their endowments and redefine their constitution. Relations between the college and Chapter became increasingly acrimonious. In March 1591 James Bisse, the sub-dean (the Dean, John Herbert, was a non-resident layman), and five residentiary canons drafted a letter to an unknown recipient who was almost certainly Bishop Thomas Godwyn. In it they thanked him for what he had done to 'reforme' the Vicars' case 'in such things as they sought against reason, conscience and the ancient government of our church'. They begged him not to allow any further alteration thereof 'as they have boasted they will procure by all the friends they have in England'. The idea that a dozen vicars choral should have more influential friends than senior cathedral clergy is a novel one. The canons went on to warn that if the vicars' attempt should be effectual in the matter, then

> 'their unbridled liberty would soon run out into all disorder and that their contemptuous pride towards those who were wont to govern them should soon be found intolerable. Besides that, how unlikely is it that a good choir should long continue when places filled by their election shall be saleable may easily be conceived. And that they are like to be doth already too plainly appear, by the unlawful dealings and detestable corruption which we have found to be amongst them that way of late'.[26]

The reference to the vicars selling appointments to their number is intriguing; little evidence of it occurs elsewhere, but that certainly does not mean it did not happen, see p. 43 for example. With an admirable degree of even-handedness, Queen Elizabeth issued two charters on 25 November 1591.[27] That granted to the Dean and Chapter was designed to found and establish the cathedral church anew with the five dignitaries of dean, precentor, archdeacon of Wells, chancellor and treasurer, three lesser dignitaries of archdeacon of Taunton, archdeacon of Bath and subdean, and a maximum of eight and minimum of six residentiary canons. These men were to form the Chapter in whom 'the rule, management and government and disposal of the affairs of the cathedral' were to be vested. The forty-nine non-residentiary prebendaries were left with an purely honorary position, their only remaining role a voice in the election of a bishop. It did not, of course, prevent them from drawing the income from their prebendal estates. The new charter granted to the vicars choral on the same day formed the basis of its constitution until the twentieth century and the end of its formal existence.

CHAPTER FOUR
REVOLUTION AND RESTORATION

The preamble of the charter granted by Queen Elizabeth to the College of Vicars Choral sets out what the vicars had always regarded as their position: they were a self-governing college with the authority to hold property, make leases and receive payments therefrom. As the charter goes on to state, 'some questions doubts and ambiguities have lately arisen and been stirred as concerning and upon the validity of the aforesaid grants, conveyances and assurances' and 'whether the aforesaid college has been duly, rightly and legitimately founded and established' was in question. Unfortunately there is no indication as to who had been doing the stirring, but the questions may have been raised by the Chapter.[1]

The charter's aim was to put an end to all the doubts and ensure the college's legal status. It was henceforth to be a corporate body with all rights to sue and be sued, grant leases and receive gifts of property. As such a body, it was to consist of two principals and five seniors elected annually, with a minimum of seven others and a maximum total of twenty members. All the vicars in post were named and the queen presented each of them to the Dean and Chapter, requiring them formally to re-admit the men to their several vicarships. At a vacancy the former were to nominate a new vicar within three months, but only if the vicars, or a majority of them, judged him suitable would he be admitted for a year's probation. At the end of this period, again only if a majority of the vicars found him 'able, sufficient and fit', was he to be perpetuated and if not he was expelled. If, after three months, the Chapter had not nominated a man, the vicars could nominate their own candidate. Once perpetuated, the vicar's position was for life unless he was lawfully deprived and the college had the power to expel an offending member. His stipend was to be £3 p.a. and the vicars were to share among themselves any stipends accumulated through vacancies.

The charter also gives a detailed description of all the property owned by the college, from which it had been receiving profits and rents for the last twenty years. The estates comprised houses, barns, stables, an inn, a watermill and nearly 800 acres of land in various Somerset parishes. Still dealing with financial matters, the charter states that the Dean and Chapter, the canons and prebendaries and every newly appointed prebendary were to pay to the vicars all the fees, wages and stipends the latter had enjoyed for the last twenty years, while in turn the vicars would pay to the Chapter any payments they had been accustomed to make. The vicars were to be subject to the jurisdiction of the Dean and Chapter everywhere except the Close, and they were to observe the statutes of Bishops Ralph and Thomas (with a hastily inserted clause excepting certain ordinances of a superstitious nature) and the bishop was to be Visitor of the college and the patron of their houses. The final provision of the charter was a new seal for the college.

The importance of the charter is underlined both by the fact that its anniversary is still celebrated and that, to mark the occasion in 1591, the vicars took the highly innovative step of commissioning a group portrait. Hanging on the east wall of Vicars' Hall is a large panel painting, not, perhaps, of great artistic merit, but of considerable historical interest, and with a curious composition.[1] The top left hand quarter shows Bishop Ralph receiving a petition from a large group of vicars, tonsured and wearing their surplices, and in return handing to them their first charter. Both the petition and the charter bear Latin verses describing Bishop Ralph's endowment of the college. While impossible to date accurately, it has a distinctly medieval look to it. The remainder of the painting is completely different. It is filled with a group of seventeen vicars wearing late Elizabethan or early Jacobean clothes, ruffs and beards, who bear no relation in size to the earlier group. The impression given is that they are individual portraits. Below them is a plaque with more Latin verse celebrating the granting of Queen Elizabeth's charter. The Latin was first translated by Dr Francis Godwin, a Wells canon who became bishop of Llandaff in 1601, thus giving a probable date of the painting as the decade between 1591 and 1601; Godwin remained a canon until 1617, but after 1601 his interest was presumably transferred to Llandaff. The painting contains 17 portraits and we have the names of all the vicars when they signed for their 1591/2 allowances; unfortunately we cannot put the names to the faces. There has certainly been subsequent over-painting, probably as a means of updating the faces as the members of the college changed.

The two charters granted by Queen Elizabeth may have defined the powers and rights of the Dean and Chapter and the college of vicars choral, but they did not necessarily resolve the difficulties between the two organisations. One was a serious dispute with the Dean and Chapter over the payments of emoluments to the vicars from the communar's fund. The charter confirmed that each vicar was to be awarded £3 from an annual sum of £76, with a proviso that if their numbers fell below twenty, then any unpaid stipend would be divided up among the existing college members. Since the usual number was about fourteen, this made a considerable difference to their incomes. The Chapter was reluctant to part with the additional money and in 1594 the college took its complaint to the Privy Council. Archbishop Whitgift was appointed to adjudicate and found in favour of the vicars, ordering that the unexpended portion of the money should be divided among them 'according to their several merits and necessities, the better to keep them in order, obedience and attendance upon their duties'.

Even this did not have the desired result, because the college had to present a second petition to the Privy Council in 1604. This time it was ordered that the vicars' stipends should be augmented by using the income from six prebendal stalls totalling £11 0s. 4d.; these were six stalls which no longer supported a vicar after the reduction in their numbers, the equivalent sums going into the cathedral's fabric fund and the considerable remaining amount going into the cathedral's common funds, to be divided among the residentiary canons. The gradual reduction in the number of canons after the Reformation also meant that the remaining ones received a much higher sum when the surplus in the common funds were divided amongst them each year, while the vicars continued to receive the fixed sum of £76. For the vicars to receive the income from six stalls, totalling more than £10, would have considerably diminished the canons' incomes from the common fund. In addition, the Privy Council directed the Dean and Chapter to divide all rents and fines from the escheatory lands formerly belonging to the cathedral chantry endowments equally among the vicars as well the canons. Although that should have been the end of the matter, the dispute rumbled on, since in March 1609, Chapter decreed that the vicars should withdraw all actions and complaints against it and submit themselves to the Chapter. Whether they did or not is unclear, but issues over the question of the escheatory remained. So did the question of stall wages. These were not the issue of the six stalls referred to above, but the basic stipend representing each vicar's payment for his services as a canon's deputy in services, and charged upon the canon in question's prebend. Stall wages varied between 20s. and 53s.4d. but most were fixed at 26s.8d. although these sums were not proportional to the value of the prebend as they had been in the past. Nothing was ever done about augmenting stall wages and defaulting prebendaries were regularly called to account. In 1614 Chapter ordered that every canon on installation enter into a bond for £40 to ensure they performed their duties properly and paid their vicar's stipend.[2]

The reluctance of the Dean and Chapter to pay the vicars the additional sums awarded to them by the archbishop's judgement was only one illustration of the financial problems they were facing. The cathedral itself was suffering from dilapidation and neglect, at least in part because of non-residential deans and canons, income from rents was stagnant and the effects of inflation, though unrecognised, were dire. In 1612 Chapter ordered all prebendaries to contribute a tithe of their income for 3 years to try and amend the ruinous state of the church, its ornaments and its bells. At the same time the college was suffering in much the same way. It was a substantial institution, with a number of employees that had to be paid. Mention was made of the cook in the previous chapter, but there would have been servants such as a laundress, brewer, porter and gardener as well. The hall was comfortably furnished, though there are only two articles from it which date from the early Stuart period, the fire-screen dated 1618 and made in the Sussex Iron Foundaries (now stored in the cathedral library muniment room) and the elm storage chest in the Exchequer, inscribed 'P.L. 1633' (whoever PL may have been, he was not a vicar choral). Wealthier vicars made gifts of silver and pewter to the College, but the communal income was not rising. Even the stagnating rents on the vicars' estates were often in arrears; in 1616 the arrears of £129 were higher than the rent receipts of £113 4s.7d. However, it is worth noting that in 1605, in an account of monies due to King James from former monastic and ecclesiastical lands, that the sum of £10 due from the bishop of Bath and Wells to the vicars choral was still payable; this of course was Bishop Ralph's original endowment of the college, its value long since eroded by inflation. College life was also stagnating in ways other than the financial. Although it had a library, it is debatable how much it was used. Most of the vicars were not highly educated and many of the existing books were in Latin. The first entry in English in the college act books dates from 28 December 1624; in it the company agreed that two of their number, James Reade and Robert Yarrow be fined two pence each for breaking the 11th statute of the house by using 'intemperate words'.[3]

The biggest effect on the college's communal life, which led inexorably to its decline, was marriage. Both priest vicars and lay vicars settled their wives in the Close; the records do not refer to the marital status of vicars, though there are occasional references to widows of vicars, mostly in need of pecuniary help. In 1612, for example, vicar Richard Mason 'dyed so poore and left his wife in such poor estat that she could not paye for his grave, ringyng the bells and other requisites for his funerall'; the Dean and Chapter stepped in and paid them for her. The existence in the Close of a predominantly lay body of men within the enclosed life of the Liberty led inevitably to disciplinary problems. In 1607 the vicars were admonished to attend church more frequently and not go out of their close into the town without their gowns. At the same Chapter meeting, vicar choral John Corne was charged with using 'very unreverent wordes of the canons of this church, viz. that he cared not a fart for any of the doctors of this church'. Despite this inauspicious beginning, Corne went on to hold several minor appointments on behalf of the Chapter. In 1609 another vicar was charged with incontinence and ordered to make public confession during Sunday Morning Prayer, standing without his surplice, to read the psalm, say a prayer and ask the congregation to pray for the amendment of his life. In this case, prayer did not work and neither did public humiliation. While the authorities were generally lenient, he was dismissed within a year. John Corne's behaviour was under the spotlight again, much later, in 1628. Mary Clarke, wife of a fellow vicar, was reported as saying that some of the ministers (by which she meant priest vicars responsible for taking many of the cathedral services) were 'whoremasters and drunkards' and named Corne and fellow vicars William and Francis Clun, from whose unworthy hands she refused to receive communion. Mary's meaning is not entirely clear, but may have referred to the performance of clandestine marriages by some of the priest vicars, where the couples in question had neither had banns read nor obtained a bishop's licence. A possible motive can be supplied by the fact that two years earlier, a feud between Mary and Agnes Corne was public enough for the two women to be summoned before Chapter for brawling in church during a service. John Corne was in trouble again in 1629 when at a Chapter meeting he said that whatever order concerning precedence the Dean and Chapter set down, he would not perform it. Denounced by one of the canons, Dr Revett, as a 'sawcie fellow', he responded 'in cholerick, angry, contemptuous and unmannerly fashion' that Dr Revett should "Call them sawcie fellows that eate of your sauce; I eate noen of it'. Corne was suspended and threatened to appeal to the bishop. While it is impossible to be certain, this may have been symptomatic of religious differences within the cathedral community.[4]

Such squabbling was probably typical of life at Wells in the first quarter of the seventeenth century, and the musical side was not immune. In February 1623 the precentor, Edward Abbott, complained to his Chapter colleagues that the choristers were not being taught properly, and he was presumably referring to their musical education rather than their schooling. Matters did not improve and the level of complaints grew. In June 1625, after receiving several warnings, the Master of the Choristers, Walter Tailer, was dismissed. He was replaced by John Okeover (or Oker, the names seem to have been interchangeable), a musician of some repute. He had arrived in Wells as a vicar choral in early 1620 and was appointed organist immediately. Thereafter musical life in Wells improved and Oker found the time to complete an Oxford degree in music in 1633. There is no surviving record of the music performed on a day by day basis, though as for earlier periods presumably music by specific composers was purchased, generally copied into in bound volumes rather than used as individual sheets. Anthem and service books were bound separately, as were organ books. Vicars commonly had their own books while the boys shared. Payments were made to 'prickers' or copyists, sometimes by the vicars themselves, if they chose not to prick their own books. It is rare to find a reference to the need for a specific voice, i.e. tenor, bass, but in 1636 Archbishop Laud recommended the employment of a particular tenor, but after being informed of the needs of the choir, graciously conceded. Many of the men who became vicars were already known to the cathedral community, but if not, they were subject to an audition. If a man was already a priest, the selection procedure was less rigorous because if he turned out to be unsuitable, he could be given a modest living elsewhere.[5]

Despite the financial struggles, life in the cathedral in the first two decades of the seventeenth century continued to run at least relatively smoothly. The death of Elizabeth marked the end of an era, but the accession of James I changed little and while there were inevitably disagreements among the clergy over theology, the Elizabethan settlement had long proved itself capable of absorbing a wide range of views. This began to change with the meteoric rise of William Laud during the early years of the reign of Charles I. Laud was made Bishop of St David's in 1621, of Bath and Wells in 1626, London in 1628 and finally Archbishop of Canterbury in 1633. He was non-resident at Wells and as far as the records reveal he made little impact there in the brief time he was bishop, but he was almost certainly responsible for a letter received by the dean in July 1632. Although signed by John Coke, it expressed King Charles' displeasure that the communion table in the cathedral was 'not furnished with such decent ornaments as are requisite and as in other cathedral churches are supplied'. The king expected a speedy redress in the matter and the cathedral authorities were charged not to neglect their duty. This was followed up in 1634 when Archbishop Laud's commissioners visited all the cathedrals in the Canterbury province. Among other charges, the cathedrals were required to maintain ' a skilful organist and able singers', as well as the full number of well-trained choristers. The cathedrals were then ordered to correct the faults that had been identified. Wells seems to have passed the musical test of Laud's commissioners, but the Dean and Chapter were commanded that they provide 'suitable ornaments for the church' and pay for them out of their dividends –

the annual surplus of receipts over disbursements, which was usually divided among the canons.[6]

Laud had continued to take an interest in the choir at Wells after his departure. In January 1635 the Dean and Chapter were hovering anxiously over his possible wish to have a boy called Francis Lewes placed as a chorister. The new bishop, William Piers, a protege of Laud, also favoured Lewes. The Chapter ordered Oker not to admit him until the archbishop expressed his pleasure, and if he did not, then since the bishop also wished it, Lewes was to be admitted, but only 'yf he be as fitt as another that shall be tendered'. There were apparently three other likely boys and 'it is right that the worthiest be chosen'. Since one of those three was named George Oker, it would be interesting to know which boy was finally chosen, but there is no further documentary evidence of any of them. At the same Chapter meeting, Oker was admonished and suspended from office for one week because he 'did not consult with the canons resident of this church before he did give notice to the vicars that there should be noe antumne sung in steede of *Nunc Dimittus* or *Benedictus*, but only according to the forme of common prayer'. Oker replied that 'he was commaunded by the reverend father in god the lord bushopp of Bath and Wells in the presence of Dr Wood, to give such notice' and no, he had not consulted or indeed informed the other resident canons. The dean, after consulting the statutes, pronounced him contumacious and passed his sentence.[7]

The cathedral had other problems relating to the vicars, or rather, their wives. In 1633 galleries had been built over the prebendal stalls in the Quire in order to provide seating during the services for the wives of the members of Chapter. Ten years later, however, because some improper persons had presumed to sit in them, the doors were nailed shut. It was regarded as particularly unsuitable for 'men and women to sitt together in so eminent a place in the view of the choyre'. It seems likely that Chapter had agreed to provide seats as well for the wives of the vicars, but 'since the ereccion of them, some of the said woemen cannot agree about their places therein'. It was therefore necessary to order the wives to 'sitt in the respective sides of the said choyre, by priesthood and seniority as their husbandes places are in, without any disturbance'. In January 1632, Joan, wife of vicar Henry Pope, was cited before Chapter for using 'irreverent and unmannerly words to Mrs Curle, the bishop's wife, in the cloister of the palace. What Joan was doing in the palace is not revealed, but Mrs Curle had complained to her that her husband Henry was the reputed father of a bastard, to which Joan's spirited response was 'Mistress Curle, you were noe bolster nor pillow, how could you tell who is the father of it?' Whatever the truth of the matter, Henry was never disciplined for it.[8] Such petty troubles in a small society were soon to give way to much more serious problems as the country sank into the mire of civil war.

For several years reformers had had the Anglican Church in their sights. They wanted the abolition of bishoprics as the start of a radical overhaul. By 1642 Laud was in the Tower and bishops had been excluded from the House of Lords. If bishops went, so too would cathedrals. Both were prime targets of Puritan emnity and had little support in Parliament. In the course of the campaign for the removal of 'popish ornaments' from churches, cathedrals were first in the firing line. At Wells, an unidentified residentiary canon left an eyewitness account of iconoclasm in the cathedral and named names. With the foresight to suspect that any papers among his possessions at home might at some point be seized, he left his account in the cathedral library, on the title page of Ludolphus's *Vita Jesu Christi*, and then simply tucked the book back into its place on the shelf. On the first occasion, in 1642, the attack was not a serious one: Richard Allen, having just been instituted to the incumbency of Batcombe, visited the cathedral with his brother, also a clergyman, and another stranger, a layman from London. While the two Allens looked on and kept watch, the layman 'most maliciously threw a stone' at a 'very faire crucifix' standing behind the Quire and smashed it. A few months later, civil war broke out. Almost exactly a year after the first attack, in April 1643, the unknown canon pulled the book off the shelf again and made another entry. This time he reported that pictures and crucifixes in the church and lady chapel were smashed before the palace was plundered and vandalised by parliamentary soldiers. A few days later, Colonel Alexander Popham's soldiers 'after dynner rusht into the church, broke the windows, organs, fonte, seates in the quire, the busshops see [sic], besides many other villanies'. The vicars seem hastily to have removed from sight the most obvious incentives to damage in their hall. The images of the Madonna and Child were excised from the arms of Glastonbury in the east oriel windows, where the darker green glass that was substituted can be discerned. Although there is no evidence for it, it would be extremely surprising if the two medieval statutes on the east wall of the hall were not discreetly removed and placed safely in storage.

Despite attacks on the cathedral, Wells was predominantly royalist in the period 1642-45 and there is little doubt that this was the sentiment of the senior clergy and their officials. The bishop, William Piers, had been imprisoned in 1640 for his Laudian policies in the diocese and although later released, then lived in semi-retirement in Oxfordshire. In January 1642 a new dean had been instituted at Wells. Walter Raleigh was a nephew of the great Elizabethan adventurer and already a Somerset incumbent and a canon as well as being one of the king's chaplains. By January 1645, he and the Chapter were contemplating the unthinkable, that it might 'heare after happen that the Corporation of the Dean and Chapter be dissolved by Act of Parliament or by other legal meanes'. If it happened, there would be little they could do except ensure that each canon would be paid back any caution money he had deposited.[9] On 28 January, a final entry was made in the Chapter act book. Clearly the orderly pattern of worship and cathedral life had become impossible. The canons, some of whom had private means, could retire quietly to their prebends, living off the income from their estate, many were also incumbents of parishes and the choristers could go home to their parents but what of the vicars choral? Their homes in the Close were apparently safe, but they had lost their entire income from the cathedral, although in theory, their canons should still have been paying them small stipends from the income of each prebend. That they did not starve was due to the custom, by now nearly a century old, of supplementing this income by taking other jobs, but some of these were inevitably in or around the cathedral and had likewise disappeared. In what was to be their last action as a corporate body for many years, they petitioned the Committee of Lords and Commons appointed for the Sequestration of Delinquents' Estates for relief. They were encouraged by the fact that the lesser clergy at St Paul's and Westminster Abbey had done likewise and had their stipends restored to them. The Wells petition was signed by ten out of the fourteen vicars (interestingly, John Oker, master of the choristers, was not one of them) and they stated that they and their families, 'some 60 poor persons' in all, 'have bin always bread in the science of Musick, and thereby not capable of any gainfull imployment' and asked for the restoration of their stipends and revenues for their lifetimes. On 13 February 1646, the Committee for Sequestrations referred their petition to the Committee for Compounding with a view to allowing the vicars stipends from the sequestered revenues of the cathedral. Alas for the vicars, the Barons of the Exchequer were still ordering further enquiries into the matter more than three years later.[10]

From 1645 the cathedral was technically closed, but for the next few years it is quite likely that some of the priest vicars were able to hold the occasional service. Details of one of them have survived. Dean Raleigh had retired to his rectory at Chedzoy, but was captured by parliamentary forces following the fall of Bridgwater in July 1645. He was in various prisons around the county for about a year until he was finally transferred to his own erstwhile deanery, where his gaoler was the county marshal, a Welshman named David Barrett. The dean applied for permission to visit his wife and children and was turned down by the county committee. He therefore informed them that their official, Barrett, was accepting bribes to free prisoners illegally on parole. Disciplined and threatened with dismissal Barrett took his anger out on the dean. Entering his chamber the next day, he found Raleigh writing to his wife and demanded to see the letter, Raleigh refused and Barrett seized it from him and drawing a knife, stabbed him in the stomach. Although the wound proved mortal, the dean lingered on for about six weeks before dying. He was buried secretly in the Quire in an unmarked grave by the dean's stall, according to the rites of the (by then illegal) Book of Common Prayer. The vicar who officiated, Francis Standish, was also the curate of St Cuthbert's and governor of the Almshouses from 1644 to 1671; he was imprisoned for a short time by the county committee, before resuming his duties at the Almshouses. If Barrett was ever held to account, it did not affect his position: he remained county marshal for the next four years.[11]

Such services as the priest vicars were able to hold came to an end in 1649. The cathedral was handed over to a Presbyterian preacher named Dr Cornelius Burges. He was owed a large sum of money by Parliament and decided to accept repayment in the form of bishops' lands. Those he got in Wells brought him into conflict with the city corporation which had also bought some of them and was claiming manorial rights that Burges regarded as his. The legal battles lasted until the Restoration in 1660. Burges bought the Deanery, Vicars' Hall, the Chapter House, and the Camery as well. In 1649 Parliament authorised the setting up of a commission to survey all church and Crown lands with a view to eventually selling off everything, not just episcopal properties, which had already been dealt with. Accordingly, the estates of the college were inspected and surveyed between March and July 1649, not by the customary method of sworn testimony by a local jury before a panel of commissioners, but a much more elaborate administrative machinery of surveyors, trustees, contractors etc.[12] The resulting survey was extremely thorough and detailed, covering 137 pages, and included revised rents based on the current market value of property. The vicars owned 103 houses, 3 barns, 5 stables, a mill and an inn, together with a total acreage of 871 acres, of which about two thirds was pasture and the rest arable, with a few gardens, orchards and woodlands. What the 1649 survey highlighted was the low rents the vicars had been receiving, in some cases unaltered since the 15th century. In the case of Cheddar, the total had been £8 5s. 2d., while the market rent was set at £82 9s. 3d. and for Newton Plecy the figures were £10 13s. 1d. and £216 10s. 6d. respectively. Even assuming that the survey was designed to wring the maximum amount out of the estates, that is an astonishing difference. Exactly what happened to the estates is not known because the college lease books, account rolls and court rolls ceased to be maintained. It may, however, be supposed that as on other ecclesiastical estates the parliamentary commissioners began the process by selling off vacant properties.

The Parliamentary Survey also gives a picture of the Close, almost exactly three hundred years after it was built. The hall and offices were valued at £110, with the adjoining kitchen, buttery and brewhouse proposed for demolition with its roof lead and slate to be sold. The survey records a total of 38 houses, twenty on the east side and eighteen on the west, only four fewer than originally built. Despite having had the right to amalgamate properties to provide houses for married vicars, it is clear that in 1649 most of the families still lived in accommodation designed in the mid 14th century for one man. The Survey describes many of the houses as 'void', even when noting the name of a tenant. For the most part, each vicar held his own living accommodation and an adjacent house, which was either void or recorded as let. The vicars' houses were each valued at a market rent of approximately 25s. p.a., while the 'void' houses were given an improved value of 13s.4d. The chapel and its chamber above were valued at 20s., but the adjoining house (now No. 14), which was the largest in the Close and occupied by vicar Henry Pope, was noted as worth 33s.4d. The most valuable was the last house nearest the gateway on the east side (now No. 1, St Andrew's Street), let to William Whiting for 2s. p.a. but worth, according to the commissioners, a rent of 43s. p.a. Except for the latter described as 'containing five low rooms and a backside and four chambers or upper rooms', the survey gives no indication of the structure or layout of any of the houses. Clearly the rents for those houses not held by individual vicars did not form a substantial part of the college income, and is another example of the lack of business skills in the running of their estate.[13]

At the time of the survey there were still twelve of the fourteen vicars living in the Close. Unless they had been fortunate enough to obtain employment elsewhere, this made sense. With no income, but free living accommodation, where else could they go? In their petition for the restoration of their stipends made in 1646, they had pitifully stated that they could do nothing but make music, but since in the past they had taken part-time jobs to eke out those stipends, it seems likely that some of them at least managed to keep body and soul together. Whether or not as a result of the survey, 1649 brought some financial relief to eight of the ten vicars who had petitioned; two, Dewbery and Mowrie, had died but their widows were still living in the Close. In November of that year, the Barons of the Exchequer ordered further enquiries, and although there is no formal record of the resumption of some form of stipend, there is evidence in 1658 that the seven remaining vicars were in receipt of small sums paid by the Trustees for the Maintenance of Ministers and were still resident in the Close.[14]

Relief finally came to the vicars and other cathedral clergy with the Restoration of Charles II to his throne in 1660. At Wells the general rejoicing was marked by the ringing of bells and the distribution of £5 to the poor in the Almshouse. Bishop Piers, one of the relatively few bishops to survive to repossess their bishoprics after the Commonwealth and Protectorate, came back to Wells. The new dean was Robert Creyghton, who had been Charles II's chaplain in exile, and within a year five new residentiary canons were appointed. It was their task to bring back both the fabric of the cathedral and its services to their former glory. Surprisingly, they were not short of money. The new leases and fines for its property after fifteen years in abeyance brought the Chapter nearly £14,000 over the next three years. However, entry fines could only be levied at the renewal of a lease, which were generally for either 21 years or three lives. In 1660 the Chapter granted well over a hundred, and it was this exceptional yield which paid for the repairs, but there followed a long dearth until those leases once more fell in. Much of this bounty found its way into the pockets of the Chapter in the form of dividends, but about £3,000 paid for restoring the building and its fittings. Of £1,084 spent on repairs in 1660, most went on timber, glass and tiles, but £400 went towards a new organ and £80 'for our little organ', presumably the one in the Lady Chapel. Money was also found for 6 vases for the communion table, 14 new Prayer Books and a 'whirlygig' for the clock. The great brass lectern now in the Retroquire, was the personal gift of Dean Creyghton; he and the bishop between them contributed £800 worth of ornaments to the cathedral.[15]

In the first list of vicars after the Restoration, which dates from April 1664, five of those who were there in 1645 remained, including Francis Standish, who had presided over the burial of Dean Ralegh. Since the others had almost certainly died rather than moved away, it indicates a remarkable degree of continuity in the Close. In 1662 John Oker, describing himself as organist after 'our late happie restauration to our places', was forced to petition the Chapter, because he had had a long and tedious illness, which had proved very expensive, and his canon owed him two years' salary (53s.4d) from the prebend of Wanstrow. In the following year, John Browne is named as organist and Oker was presumably dead; his widow Mary continued to receive payments on behalf of her son, another John, who was a chorister.[16]

If the Chapter had received considerable windfalls from their estates from new entry fines, it might reasonably be supposed that the vicars benefited similarly. They took back control over their estates soon after the Restoration and the first manorial court thereafter took place at Dulcote on 24 January 1661. This was the best chance the college would ever have to put its estate management on a more profitable and businesslike footing. The vicars were in dire financial straits, needing money to repair and restore their properties in the Close. The estate rents, largely unchanged since the 15th century and taking no account of inflation in the interim, had undoubtedly been increased by the landlords who had acquired their properties during the Commonwealth period, even if not by the spectacular margins recommended by the Parliamentary Survey. Now was their chance to revalue their properties and when the leases fell in, increase the rents to something more akin to the going rate as well as charging realistic entry fines for the granting of new leases. They also had the option of changing the ancient copyhold custom of leases for 3 lives, renewable on payment of a fine whenever one of the named lives died and a new one was added, into a fixed term lease, usually 21 years, which would enable them to review rents at regular intervals, or if they chose to retain the old custom, at least not renewing any of the leases until all the lives had run out and then re-leasing at improved rents. True to form, the College failed to act and the opportunity was lost.[17]

In 1663 the financial position was so desperate that on 15th June the vicars choral petitioned Bishop Piers, their Visitor, and the petition gives some indication of what happened in the Close during the 1650s. '..all the lands & houses of the Corporacions of the Vicars Chorall and petty Canons belonging to the Catheddrall Churches were sold awaye & the purchasers of them did goe on to demolish theire homes & to sell the materialls thereof amongest which your petitioners did extremely suffer & were turned out of doores plundred & imprisoned & were reduced to greate want and poverty untill it pleased God to restore this Land to her ancient & flourishing estate by the Restauracion. Your petitoners (blessed be God) doe nowe enjoye their homes lands and Colledge againe. But in the tymes of the late troubles most of our houses in Close hall were defaced, uncovered & extreme ruinated which neither we the nowe vicars Chorall nor our Successors are any wise able to rebuild or repaire haveing but a quarter yearely maintenance for us & our families & haveing noe Benefactores nor likely to have any help us in this case'. What the vicars wanted of the bishop was his formal permission to lease out twelve of the most decayed houses for the term of 21 years to persons of 'goode & honest reputations as will covenant to rebuilde them at their owne proper Coste', paying no fines and very low rents.[18]

The petition begs a number of questions. The first section reads as though it was a standard document used by a number of similar organisations. There is no firm evidence that any of the Wells vicars had been forcibly evicted, or, apart from Francis Standish, imprisoned, or any of the Close Hall houses completely demolished. The latter were undoubtedly in very poor condition, however, and this was a sensible way of ensuring the worst were properly repaired. The 1649 Survey showed quite clearly that each of the fourteen vicars held their own and an adjoining house, and these were either let, empty, or in a few cases amalgamated into their own living accommodation. The petition does not mention letting any of these on repairing leases, which might have been expected if they were all in a poor state, stating instead that each vicar might have a double house, one for his habitation and the other for his 'necessities'; what these were is not clear but almost certainly its practical implication was 'rent money'. Those that were let were presumably by private arrangement and the rent taken by the vicar concerned rather than by the college. The twelve houses not held by individual vicars that were to be let formally were scattered among the rest and must be repaired or 'else the whole fabricke will have breaches and thother houses wil be in danger by windes or otherwise beinge without the support of the rest'. This does not suggest that in 1663 there were any that had yet collapsed. The solution of repairing leases seems to have worked, but was also responsible for gradual loss of uniformity in the Close houses. The street gradually became a desirable place to live for gentlefolk, particularly for clergy widows, and it was the tenants rather than the vicars who inserted more modern windows and doors. The tenants also paid small sums for local amenities: one shilling a year for the Scavenger (who disposed of the rubbish) and two shillings for the use and maintenance of the two wells, one at each end of the Close. The house in the north-east corner of the Close was still ruinous in 1670 when a resident in College Lane, now North Liberty, took it on with the agreement that he should be permitted to breach the wall, giving him convenient access from the north, but destroying the integrity of the college layout.[19]

Although minor in comparison with the state of the Close, the vicars also had to face the cost of re-stocking the communal property of the hall. Its silver had been lost, presumably under the Commonwealth, but it was not just the valuables that had gone, they had to purchase replacement tankards and plates, bowls and spoons. Much of their significant collection of pewter was purchased in this period, most of it made in Bristol; the two surviving pairs of large candlesticks are rare and important.[20] New silver, including a fine chalice of 1672, came in the form of gifts, like the dish with a large flat rim with an inscription marking it as the gift of Augustin Benford in 1670. An inventory of the goods and chattels belonging to the college, drawn up in 1677 shows that by this date, its silver collection comprised as well 1 tankard, 1 bowl, 1 great salt cellar, 2 small salt cellars and 2 tumblers, all apparently gifts from the chancellor of the diocese, Dr John Baylie, as well as 2 more little salts, given by Henry Winchcombe, himself a vicar, and 2 spoons, donor unknown, and safely stored away in the Exchequer. The furnishings in the Hall included 1 table board, 4 settles, 5 joint stools, an organ, 'the king's arms', presumably a painted board, 1 large and 1 small pair of iron dogs for the hearth and in the Buttery, 1 bin, presumably the medieval bread bin, 1 cupboard and one table board. The kitchen housed all the pewter, linen, kitchen utensils etc.

In its financial straits, the college returned once more to the vexed question of the vicars' share of the escheatory, or former chantry, lands. In January 1670, Nicholas Dowthwaite, clerk of the Chapter's courts, was told to hand over to the vicars certain documents relating to their affairs which they wished to examine. This was to be done under the supervision of two of the Chapter. Immediately afterwards, Chapter decided to propose that the vicars should withdraw yet another petition which they had laid before the Archbishop of Canterbury and that both parties should disclose their cases and lay them jointly before learned counsel for an opinion in the hope that the dispute between them could be finally laid to rest. Chapter even volunteered, without prejudice, to pay the legal costs. Unfortunately, as with so many other legal cases, the records do not reveal the outcome.[21]

In the absence of the College's own records for this period, information on vicars comes only from Chapter material. As already noted, John Oker was briefly restored to his position as organist at the Restoration, but died shortly thereafter. He was succeeded by John Browne, whose tenure of the post – he died in 1674 – was not worthy of further mention in the Chapter records, but his successor, John Jackson, was paid £1 in 1681 for composing a service, with an extra £1 as a reward and in the following year, 40s. for his pains in securing services for the choir. Several of his anthems survive in the cathedral collection of part books. Jackson was also briefly master of the choristers as well, but then handed over that part of his responsibilities to Gabriel Greene in about 1680. In January 1684 Greene and John Cooper, another vicar choral, appeared before the bishop in the Chapter House and confessed that 'they had offended God Almighty and broken the king's lawes, by affronting Mr William Piers, son of the reverend Dr William Piers, late canon residentiary of this church, deceased, and riotously assaulting his man in his roome at the Miter Tavern'. They apologised humbly to all concerned, were warned to behave themselves and as a sign of penitence they were told to receive the sacrament in the cathedral on the morrow. It was particularly shameful behaviour on the part of Greene, who as master of the choristers, was expected to set an example to his charges; he finally relinquished his post in 1694 on the grounds of age and infirmity.[22]

Following John Jackson's death, Robert Hodge, who had become a vicar choral in 1687, was appointed organist in his place. It must have seemed like a good idea at the time. Hodge had been a chorister at Exeter and had appeared so promising a talent that the Exeter Dean and Chapter approved an arrangement whereby he was to be taught by someone from the Chapel Royal. His tutor there was no lesser person than Henry Purcell. In 1686 Purcell, having already forked out for a winter coat for Hodge, then found himself obliged to write to the Exeter authorities about the large number of debts the young man had contracted, many to men too poor to be able to sustain such charity; possibly Purcell was one himself. Exeter paid the debts and got small thanks for it. In early 1687 Hodge deserted their choir and became a vicar at Wells. In his probationary year he was reprimanded for breaking windows, but such was his talent that he was appointed organist in April 1688 with a stipend of £5 per quarter. He was still in Wells in April 1690, but in July of that year, his place as vicar was declared vacant 'by the going off of Mr Robert Hodge, late vicar and organist'.[23]

In March 1685 the bishop [the newly appointed Thomas Ken] and clergy of the diocese sent a humble address to the new king, the Roman Catholic James II, on his succession to his brother, Charles II. While pledging loyalty in suitably adulatory terms, it makes a pointed reference to 'the auspicious promise that your majesty has made us of protecting our establish't religion, the greatest concern we have in this world'. Religious differences were already stirring within Somerset and the Chapter had in the previous year accepted a ruling that in future no dissenter should be permitted to lease Chapter lands. When the Protestant duke of Monmouth, King Charles II's bastard son, raised the flag of rebellion against his uncle the king, it was in Somerset that he gathered most of his forces, and dissenters flocked to join him. The Chapter was quick to contribute £100 to the commander of the county militia, and it is hardly surprising that rebels in Wells attacked the cathedral as a symbol of the establishment. The aged chancellor, Thomas Holt, recorded in the Chapter Act Book 'the barbarity of the rebel fanatics, who early this very morning [1 July 1685] profaned the whole furniture thereof, almost ruined the organ, and they have transformed the sacred edifice into stalls for their horses'. One of the rebel commanders, Lord Grey, magnanimously posted himself in front of the altar, lest sacrilege be committed. While a silver virge was stolen, the sacrist James Williams managed to hide the communion silver, and Mrs Frideswide Creyghton, wife of the precentor, handed over £20 as protection money to save the canons' houses from being ransacked.[24] There is no evidence of any vicar becoming involved in the rebellion, indeed it was hardly likely when their livelihood was dependent on the established church. The battle of Sedgemoor, fought on 6 July, was an overwhelming defeat for the rebels. Many of them were brought back to the cathedral as prisoners, herded into the cloisters to await their turn for sentencing at Judge Jefferies' Bloody Assizes. The reaction of individual vicars to all this is not known. Once any damage had been made good, the life of the cathedral and its vicars settled down to the long period of somnolence that was Anglican life in the eighteenth century.

CHAPTER FIVE
STAGNATION AND COMPLACENCY?

The eighteenth century opened with Chapter dealing with a perennial problem. In 1700 two of the more senior vicars, both of them priests, Eldridge Aris and Nathaniel Brown, who had 'for some time bin absent and neglected the service in the quire .... be immediately called to residence etc. to attend and do their severall duties in the quire'. No penalty was imposed on this occasion, but such a lack of responsibility from vicars who should have been setting an example sets the tone for the decades to come. Aris should certainly have known better, for his father and namesake was vicar of Cheddar and a prebendary, but perhaps he mended his ways, for he continued to be a vicar until his resignation in October 1722. When that happened, the vicars were immediately plunged into a dispute. As his replacement, Chapter proposed Edward Johnson. Nine of the vicars agreed, but Farwell Perry, one of the two senior vicars taking their turn as principals for the year, refused to let his fellows into the hall or call a meeting to confirm the appointment. The second principal called a meeting elsewhere, and Aris' resignation was accepted and Johnson admitted on probation. Perry was suspended from all emoluments and fees for two months. This was extended until April 1723 'for his great neglect of duty and contemptuous conduct' and at the Chapter meeting in April he was dismissed. Perry promptly appealed to the bishop, who asked the Chapter which day it would be convenient to them to hear the appeal, but there is no record of the hearing or its judgement. It was not the first time Perry had been found wanting in his conduct. In July 1718 he had been admonished for neglect of his duty and on that occasion, all the vicars were summoned into the Chapter House and the dean read them a set of injunctions which neatly encapsulate the duties of the 18th century vicars.

First thing in the morning (remembering that the canons only conducted services on special feast days) the priest vicar whose turn it was to read morning prayer in the Lady Chapel was expected to be there before the bell had done tolling, wearing his canonical habit beneath his surplice and the fact that the vicars were now told that they must deliberately and devoutly read the whole of the service suggests that this was not always happening. Next, at ten in the morning and three in the afternoon they were to be in their stalls in the choir, again before the bells had finished chiming, especially the priest vicar whose office it then was to read prayers. Priest vicars were expected to come into the choir always wearing their canonical habit and surplice, and the hoods proper to their degrees. All vicars, both priests and lay, were to behave themselves seriously and devoutly in the time of divine service and perform carefully their several parts in it according to rule and order. No vicar of either sort was to presume upon any pretence whatsoever to be absent from the choir in the hours of prayer without asking and obtaining leave from the dean. At their entrance to the Quire all vicars were to conform themselves according to the ancient statute, *de ingressu clericorum*. And lastly, they all of them in their whole behaviour were to be exemplary, sober and religious, so as not to dishonour the cathedral church or discredit religion, in the service of which they are so immediately concerned. The list of what should be done clearly indicates what had not been happening, but it is interesting to note that no mention is made of the vicars' prime purpose – as singers. There presumably, they were not at fault if they bothered to turn up in the first place. The fact that Perry was dismissed five years later for neglect of duty suggests that the behaviour of vicars had not greatly improved in the interim. Nor was he the only one; only six months later Chapter again warned the vicars that they must not omit being at prayers, unless they have leave of the dean or senior canon resident and nor were they to go out of town without such leave. In July 1720 three vicars were suspended from commons for a week for absenting themselves from service the day before without leave and in November 1722, Mr Hill was dismissed, 'for neglecting for a long time to do his duty and attend as a vicar at divine service in the cathedral and for contemptuously refusing to appear before the Chapter and receive an admonition to that purpose'.[1] It is hard to believe that the attention of vicars to their duty improved much throughout the century, yet among all the admonitions there is not a single mention of their singing being at fault.

Chapter had dealt with a rather more unusual issue right at the beginning of the century. Mary Rogers, wife of George Rogers, one of the vicars, had been married by a licence of the Dean and Chapter at the end of October 1699, but had given birth to a child at the beginning of March 1700. Hardly an uncommon situation, but Chapter obviously thought vicars should set a better moral example. Mary admitted the facts but said that she and her husband had been married two years previously by the late minister of Berrow, but without banns, licence or witnesses and had no marriage certificate. For reasons known only to themselves, they had concealed this marriage and were afterwards married again in the cathedral. Given that they were legally married before the birth of their child, it is curious that the authorities pursued this issue unless they were in fact taking action against the former minister at Berrow.

Clandestine marriages were a serious problem in the eighteenth century, the most notorious of which were 'Fleet marriages' in London, conducted by bogus priests that had no legality whatsoever. In seventeenth century Wells, one of the vicars had been married to a widowed Roman Catholic by a recusant priest; although he was reprimanded, the legality of his marriage does not seem to have been questioned, nor did it apparently harm his career because he held various Chapter offices and was then presented to a benefice. Chapter was more concerned about their own vicars conducting clandestine marriages. When conducted by priest vicars (who would have pocketed a fee), marriages were clandestine if they were performed somewhere other than a church, secretly without witnesses or any public proof that the ceremony had in fact taken place. In 1719, for example, Samuel Hill (who was not a vicar choral) irregularly married Elizabeth Morris, daughter of Dr Claver Morris, who was under age and acting without her parents' consent, to John Burland, a member of the local gentry, by a licence which was invalid in Wells. Hill was subsequently forbidden to serve in the cathedral again 'on any pretext', and Thomas Cooper, the sacrist, who had assisted, was suspended for a year. To avoid any such temptation, in 1736 Chapter forbade the celebration of marriages in the Close chapel, and deemed that any such in future would be regarded as illegal; this suggests that perhaps the chapel had been used for irregular marriage services. On the other hand, in 1732 three of the priest vicars reported to Chapter that the bishop had forbidden them to conduct a marriage in the cathedral with a licence from anybody save himself. To this the Dean and Chapter took exception and ordered the priest vicars to continue marrying on licenses from them as they had done hitherto. Finally, Hardwicke's Marriage Act of 1753 dealt with the problem at a national level, when it was made clear to all clergy that marriages had to take place in a church or chapel and were illegal without banns or a bishop's licence.

The several priest vicars – and their number fluctuated since it was no longer a necessity for vicars to be in orders – were treated as curates of the cathedral and were frequently employed to carry out baptisms as well as marriages, visitation of the sick, burials and churching of women in addition to their regular duties of conducting services. The fees for such services were supposed to be equally distributed among the priest vicars, but hardly surprisingly, this was not a system which functioned well and in 1736 Chapter ordered that the services should be undertaken only by the vicar whose turn it was to read morning prayers and he was to retain the fees.[2] If such fees augmented the income of those vicars who were priests, the most common source of additional income for lay vicars was employment by the Chapter. Early in the century, 1706, a list of duties for the sacrist and three clerks includes those for the sub-treasurer, an office often held by vicars, in this case William Broderip. He was paid 40s. p.a. to take care of all the plate and vestments of the canons, provide wax for the Chapter leases at his own charge and put the seals on, receiving 2s.6d. for each lease, to provide the bread and wine for every communion at the cost of the Dean and Chapter, to take care of the altar linen, receiving 2s. p.a. for its washing, and take care of the branch and candlesticks. The more menial tasks of sweeping the cathedral, lighting candles, ringing bells and locking up fell to the sacrist and his assistant clerks or virgers. An extra 40s p.a. was a useful sum to have. The schoolmaster received the same as keeper of the library, but the cataloguing of the books was undertaken by James Nooth in 1711, again for 40s. Nooth was clearly a man of many parts because by 1719 he was deputy clerk of the courts and gamekeeper for the manor of Canon Grange, the Chapter's property in Wells.

In 1699 Henry Mills had been appointed as master of the grammar school, a position he held until April 1712 when he walked out to become master of another school in Croydon. The Dean and Chapter were indignant at the dereliction which left the school with 'no one to take care of it and the said school is now actually void', which suggests that at this period there was no under-master. The chancellor hastily used his patronage to appoint a new master. This was Robert Creyghton, M.A. A generation or so earlier, Bishop Creyghton had ensured that his son and namesake was appointed to the office of precentor, a post he filled for a record length of time, 1674-1734. The new schoolmaster was probably a grandson of the precentor. He held the post until 1727 when he was presented to the vicarage of Burnham and subsequently became a prebendary. This was not the usual career path for the schoolmaster and is indicative of the widespread nepotism which characterised church life in the eighteenth century.[3] Precentor Creyghton, it should be said, was not an unworthy holder of his office. Like his father before him, he was professor of Greek at Cambridge (1666-1674) a post he gave up on becoming precentor; he had been a prebendary since 1667. He was generous to the vicars, leaving them an annual sum of £20; his contemporary, Dean Bathurst (1670-1704) endowed them with an equal amount. Creyghton was both musical and an amateur composer, and more than a dozen of his works, anthems and service settings, survive in the cathedral part books. In these books, the music of Creyghton and his predecessor, John Jackson, is the earliest music written by Wells men that survives in the cathedral archives.[4]

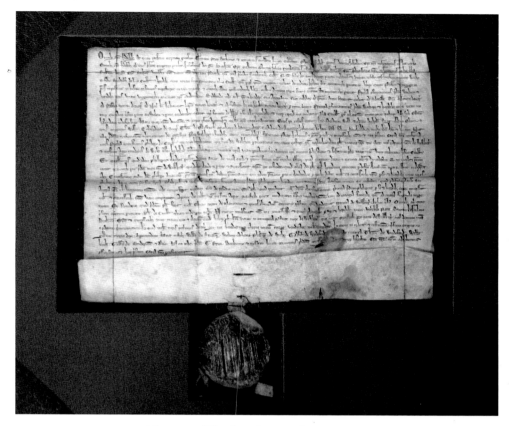

Figure 1: *The foundation charter, 1348*

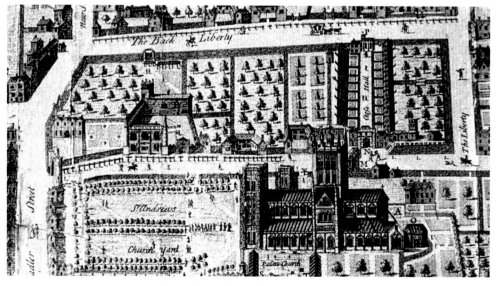

Figure 2: *The Liberty by William Simes, 1735 [detail]*

Figure 3: Tomb of Bishop Ralph of Shrewsbury, d. 1363

Figure 4: Vicars' Hall

Figure 5: *Carved wooden figures in the Hall*

Figure 6: *The medieval bread cupboard*

Figure 7: Stained glass image of St Katherine in the Hall

Figure 8: Medieval music sheet [detail]

Figure 9: *No. 22 Vicars' Close, the least altered medieval house*

Figure 10: *Effigy of Bishop Thomas Bekynton, d. 1465*

Figure 10: *View down the Close showing the 15th century administrative block*

Figure 11: View of the Close from the Muniment room

Figure 12: The steward's room or exchequer

Figure 13: The medieval multi-draw cabinet in the Muniment room

Figure 14: *The Chapel and Library*

Figure 15: *The Chain Gate*

Figure 16: The 15th century face of the clock, opposite the vicars' kitchen window

Figure 17: Octagonal chimney shaft added to the original base of the stack

Figure 18: Richard Pomeroy's fireplace and lectern

Figure 19: A large cooking pot with some of the 17th century pewter

Figure 20: *The Close in the early 19th century*

Figure 22: *The Chapel in the early 19th century*

Figure 23: Burges's Gothic Dresser, displaying some of the 17th century pewter

Figure 24: The Close from the Gateway

Figure 25: The Wall Painting in No. 9 Vicars' Close

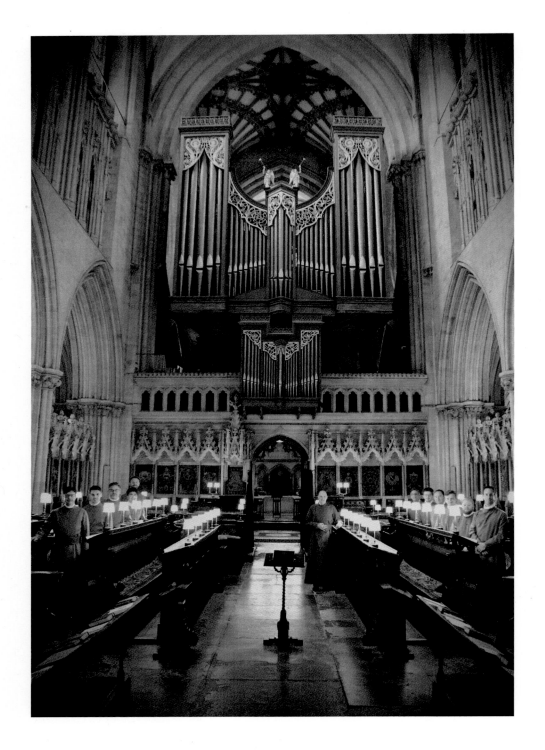

Figure 26: *Vicars Choral in the Quire*

Creyghton's music was regarded rather more highly in the eighteenth century than would be the case now. Burney, writing in 1789, expressed the view that 'though he was not gifted with great original genius for musical composition .... yet he has left such pleasing proofs of his progress in the art as manifest judgement, taste and knowledge', and in 1834 William Bingley observed of his anthem "I will arise and go to my father" that 'no-one can peruse it without regretting that it should be so short'. In contrast, writing in 1972, Long described the same work as 'a pedantic, somewhat stilted little work ... It is dangerously easy to write a contrived canon as a technical exercise, but so very difficult to write one which is also inspired music, artistically satisfying'. Somewhat lesser in standing was Anthony Walkeley, a third generation vicar choral, who went on to become organist at Salisbury cathedral at the beginning of the eighteenth century, but whose anthems and services were purchased for use at Wells.[5]

The lack of the College's own act book for the first half of the 18th century is to some extent compensated by other sources of information not available in earlier times. One of the best for Wells is the diary of a physician called Claver Morris. The son of a vicar in Dorset, he settled in Wells in about 1685, where he ran a successful medical practice, held various public offices and was an enthusiastic amateur musician, who owned and could presumably play, a number of instruments. It is from Morris's diary that we learn that as well as repairing the organs in the cathedral and St Cuthbert's, Thomas Swarbrick also repaired the organ in Vicars' Hall, 'adding a bassoon and Hoboy stop and sinking the pitch a lesser third to bring it nearer concert pitch', for which, and for personally lowering it a note, he was paid £25. The reason for the existence of an organ in Vicars' Hall is that soon after his arrival in Wells, Morris began a music club which met there every Tuesday for many years; a gallery was even erected for their instruments. No club of this nature could exist or meet in their hall without the active engagement of the vicars, many of them talented musicians as well as singers. While there is no means of judging the standard of playing, Morris owned music works ranging from Byrd to Handel and often makes a note of the music played. Members of the club ranged from the vicars and local townspeople to visiting gentry. Nor was the membership exclusively male; Morris occasionally refers to female members.[6]

Dr Morris, whose brother-in-law was a prebendary, was on social terms with both bishop and canons. For several years in the 1690s after the death of his first wife, he carried on a courtship with the daughter of Bishop Kidder, though in the end she turned him down at her father's insistence and he remarried elsewhere. In 1699 he built himself a smart new house in the Liberty, but he was also a tenant of the vicars for a stable in College Lane and several acres of land at Dulcote. More importantly, he became a sub-tenant of two houses in the Close. This was to cause much trouble in the years to come and led to a major falling out with members of the college which by 1725 ended in a legal dispute.[7] This had the sad effect of bringing the music club in the Hall to an end, though it reconvened at the Mitre Inn without the participation of the vicars. Morris died just over a year later in March 1727 and with him a wonderful informal source for life in and around Wells in the first quarter of the 18th century.

In his tour of Great Britain in 1724-6, Daniel Defoe described the clergy of Wells as 'living very handsomely' and 'there is no want of good company'. In fact the Chapter was a comfortable, self-perpetuating oligarchy, with much intermarrying among members. Since its constitution permitted the co-option of suitably qualified prebendaries into the small number of canons residentiary when vacancies occurred, this cosy arrangement meant it was not difficult to provide for relatives by blood or marriage. The only hurdle to be overcome was the right of the bishop to appoint the archdeacon and chancellor. A similar pattern can be discerned among the vicars, where two or three generations of the same family became first choristers and then vicars. The prime example was the Broderip family. William was admitted as a probationary vicar in 1701, when he was seventeen; he was appointed sub-treasurer by the Chapter in 1706 (as noted above) and following the death of John George, took up the post of organist in 1713. Several of his compositions have survived including an anthem written to celebrate the Peace of Utrecht in 1713 – not quite in the same league as the *Te Deum* composed by Handel for the same occasion. On the death of the master of choristers, Thomas Webb, in 1716, he combined the two posts. In 1720 he was reimbursed £1 11s.6d. for anthems bought of Mr Paul of Exeter, one of several similar payments. William died in 1727 and was ill enough during the last year of his life for Chapter to take the hitherto unprecedented step of paying Joseph Millard £2 2s. to play the organ in his place, unprecedented because he was not a member of the College. He continued to fill in after Broderip's death until William Evans was appointed organist. Millard finally became a vicar choral in 1738. Evans seems to have been a composer in a small way; the Chapter paid him £3 9s. 6d. for the composition of a service, which had been approved by Precentor Creyghton. Early on during Evans's period as organist, the accounts note that choir books had been stolen – the bellman was paid to cry the theft, and a considerable sum, £5 11s., had to be paid for Dr

Aldrich's and Dr Creyghton's services to be copied out again so that they could continue to be used.[8]

William Broderip had at least ten children by his wife Martha and at his death in 1727 she was granted a pension of ten shillings a week by Chapter to support herself and her family.[9] There was no regular form of pension for aged vicars (or indeed anywhere else in the Church of England); most of them continued in office until they died. One of William and Martha's sons, Edmund, became an organist in Bristol, another, John, became a vicar at Wells in 1740 and in early in 1741, before he was perpetuated, was appointed organist and master of the choristers on the death of William Evans. He was paid the usual salaries, that is, £20 p.a. as organist and £7 as master. The younger Broderip was a prolific composer and three volumes of his music were published in his lifetime. Several service settings, ranging in complexity, can be found in the part books and Barnes considers them 'representative of the generally insipid compositions for the Anglican church that were then in vogue, owing much of their harmonic and rhythmic interest to the influence of Handel.' However, much of Broderip's music took the form of psalm-settings and anthems and here 'his use of word-painting is excessive, on occasion to the point of absurdity. His rhythmic and harmonic language is unimaginative above a basic level, and his use of counterpoint is dull. Much of his music is written for treble voices, from which it may be concluded that he was a reasonable choir-trainer.' Barnes's judgement on Broderip's music may be harsh, but in Wells's terms he was a diligent choir master who composed prolifically for his choir and it was a position he occupied for thirty years. The composing was not entirely for musical reasons, since it supplemented his salary: in 1741 he was paid £1 11s. for 'writing anthems and services for the church' and in 1745, a pound for 'writing the organ part of his *Benedicite*', all useful additions to his salary. While it might be considered that these tasks were an intrinsic part of his job and it is surprising to find them additionally remunerated, it is perhaps worth noting that any of the canons residentiary or prebendaries who preached particular sermons were also handsomely rewarded at the rate of one pound per sermon.[10]

It is clear that in the first half of the 18th century, the more diligent members of Chapter were struggling against a strong laissez-faire attitude among the non-clerical members of the cathedral organisation. Chapter did its best to keep up the fabric, ordering repairs to the bells, the nave vaults and the organ, re-paving the choir and giving the walls of the body of the church a new coat of limewash. Two new galleries were erected on the north and south sides of the Quire for the use of the canons' families and seats on the north side between the door leading to the north aisle and the steps of the altar for the use of the mayor, aldermen and common council of Wells to sit and hear divine service in the 1740s. Yet in 1724 James Bacon, the junior clerk (or virger) had to be reprimanded for keeping horses and sheep in the Palm Churchyard and allowing them to come into the church and cloisters. The vicars' attitude to strict attendance at services is well-documented and in 1726 a rail had to be ordered to be erected 'from the small west door of the cathedral to the west cloister door to prevent the playing of ball there against the church wall'. This was probably aimed at the choristers, but perhaps some of the younger vicars also enjoyed ball games. In 1724 Chapter agreed to pay Thomas Swarbrick, organ maker, the large sum of £146 for major repairs to the organ and to give him a retainer of £8 to continue to carry out running repairs. Swarbrick was a German whose real name was Schwarbrook and who was based at Warwick, though he was a frequent visitor to Wells. Twelve years later, William Evans, the organist, complained that the organ was much out of repair and that Swarbrick, though often sent for, had neglected to appear. He suggested that John Harris, organ builder, was willing to do the same and Chapter ordered Mr Harris to come and survey the organ and set out his terms and proposed repairs. Nevertheless, Swarbrick continued to receive his stipend and in 1740-1 was awarded five guineas 'on account of his extraordinary trouble about the organ'.[11]

Complaints against the vicars for non-attendance in the Chapter Act Books die out in the second half of the century, but this is probably a reflection of the increasingly mechanical and less informative keeping of the books. The vicars' Act Book which begins in 1748 is only marginally better. The great majority of the entries simply record the annual election of the principals and other officers and the admission and perpetuating of the college members. Occasionally estate business occurs: in 1748 all the vicars signed an agreement that on the death of any of their number, his executors and assigns should have his dividend of any fines paid on the renewal of leases for one year after his death, minus any debts due to other vicars. While this was a reaffirmation of what had long been the case, it seems that each new vicar had to sign such an agreement because in 1776 it was decreed that the administrators of the late vicar, the Revd. Richard Hughes, were not entitled to receive his share of fines because Hughes had signed no act to thus entitle him. Any fines falling due would therefore only be divided among the other vicars. One of them, the Revd. Kymer presumably regarded this as unjust because he refused his share, saying he would appeal to the visitor, that is, the bishop.[12]

In April 1754 the vicars carried out a survey of all their estates, using the 1649 survey as a basis. The acreage had increased from 869 to 941 in the intervening century and rents now brought in just over £133 p.a. The assessments of the market value of the estates and the rents that ought to be payable was very similar to that of 1649, and would in theory have increased the rental to £693, but again nothing was done to try and increase the rents as leases fell in. It was clear that some of the tenants at least, were struggling to pay even the customary low ones. Another agreement, signed by all present at a hall meeting in 1765 was to serve notice on James Birch of Cheddar, a tenant who was in severe arrears with his rent, and levy a distress on his goods. Seven years later, Mr Witherll, the steward, was ordered to file a bill in 'His Majesty's High Court of Chancery of the Exchequer' against Birch for rent arrears of 15s. 2d. p.a., though the number of years worth of arrears is not given; it must have been substantial to justify the legal expenses of Chancery. If the land was in Cheddar itself [neither the bargain books or lease books contain any reference to a lease of Birch's as far back as 1750], the vicars' estate there was small and scattered, comprising a total of 106 acres and 20 houses, but with 27 tenants, only one of whom held more than ten acres; much the highest rent was paid for the estate mill. Most, therefore, were subsistence farmers faced with agricultural depressions brought about by severe weather or cattle plagues, who often found it difficult to pay their rents, and were not in a position to take advantage of periods of agricultural prosperity or the advances in farming techniques. Whether the expense of a court action was justified and the vicars were able to collect the arrears is undocumented.[13]

The vicars' annual accounts for most of the 18th century list their estates under the group headings of the manors of Cheddar, Kingstone, Martock and Newton Plecy; the manors of Wells, Wellesley and Dulcot which incorporated properties in Chamberlain Street, East Walls, Grope Lane, High Street, Mount Roy Lane, Southover, Tor Lane and Tucker Street, of which the 3 properties in the High Street, which included the Christopher Inn, brought in much the highest rents, Croscombe and Dinder and finally Polsham and Pennard. Although the formal annual assessment of the estate income was £133, that was not always the sum that came into the receiver's hands; occasionally there were additional sums or fines, paid on the renewal of a lease, more often tenants were in arrears. Two annual payments of £20 in dividends from bequests to the vicars by Dean Bathurst and Precentor Creyghton, together with one or two other sums which came in regularly and were listed under the heading of Perquisites & Gifts, came to just over £50. In 1739 the year's income for the college was £179 3s. 8d. Expenditure was £170 17s. 8d. which covered the payment of various taxes, such as land tax and poor rates, the payment of the steward and bailiffs and the small sums paid to the principals and receiver for that year. Each vicar received a payment of £1 p.a. to augment his stipend and £5 6s. (2s. per week) for commons from college funds in addition to their payments from the Dean and Chapter. Expenditure on the hall, close and chapel was entered in the accounts under the title of 'Great Account'. There were no longer many college servants to pay, though Betty Lane served as housekeeper for many years, and for a number of years at the turn of the century Nurse Phear, with her own house in the close, was employed, though who required nursing services is not named. Food and drink had only to be bought in for feasts on special occasions, because life was no longer communal and the hall seems to have been cleaned only occasionally, but linen was washed, knives were ground and beer was brewed and in 1704 a thousand tiles were bought for 'putting in the buttery'. The lack of communal dining did not mean that the hall was not regularly used. The vicars paid considerable sums for coals to heat it, and for candles, pipes and tobacco, suggesting that it functioned much like a gentlemen's club. The Close Hall pumps were repaired on an almost annual basis, and running repairs to the hall occur most years, with some occasional major works. In 1702, 4 bushels of hair were purchased, probably to add to plaster when the hall and exchequer were refurbished, together with thirteen sacks of lime for whitewashing. In the following year, £3 16s. was paid for a large load of tiles and the tilers seem to have been at work for several weeks, though where they were working was not specified; it was almost certainly either the hall or offices. They were busy again in 1739 and in 1781 at work on the chapel. There are also several payments for repairing windows in the hall and chapel. If there was a surplus in the accounts, as in 1739 when there was £8 6s., it was divided between the vicars rather than put in a fund towards major repair work.[14] In day to day terms, the college balanced its books. It is quite clear, however, that nothing was saved to cover unforeseen circumstances such as repairs to the hall.

It was during the 18th century that the Close became a desirable place for respectable gentlefolk to live. The houses were small, attracting widows and other single people, but had the cachet of being part of the Liberty. It was the tenants, by and large, who modernised the medieval houses, putting in new windows and doors. There are occasional references in the Vicars' Act Book to life in the Close. In 1759 Mrs Pope gave the hall a brass pot and cover (that it had a 14 inch diameter was carefully noted). In 1773 the vicars unanimously agreed that in future none of them should be obliged individually to pay for the entertainment on 8 November, but that up to £4 should be paid by the Receiver out of the common funds and that no vicar would invite any outsider to dine on that day. This refers to the annual celebration held to mark Bishop Ralph's granting of their charter in 1348, which it appears the members of the college had taken it in turns to fund. This would have been a considerable financial burden and it is not surprising members were looking for an alternative. All the estate rents were due to be paid by the beginning of November each year, so the receiver would have been holding enough funds to cover the cost of the entertainment. In January 1773 the hall meeting agreed that the great gate at the entrance to the Close was always to be kept locked and a new lock and key purchased; normal access was via the adjacent pedestrian gate, so any carts or carriages wishing to enter had to seek formal permission to do so. In 1786 the Close Hall gates were replaced, and the sale price of the old ones, four shillings, went straight into the vicars' dividend for that year. In 1770 it was noted that one of the vicars had agreed to repair the lead gutter between his house and that of one of his fellow vicars, and a few years later Mr Hunt, one of the vicars, was to have some timber cut down on the Dulcote estate for repairs to his house. The cutting of timber was a jealously guarded prerogative of the estate owner and for any other purpose than repairs on the estate itself formal permission had to be sought, even for a house in the Close. The college accounts were audited each year on 20 December and all the members were supposed to be present, but it is clear that some at least of the vicars did not bother to turn up. In 1779 it was felt necessary to rule that provided proper notice was given, any vicar who failed to attend without good reason would pay a fine of 3s.4d. and double that if he were a principal.

In the 1790s Aaron Foster, one of the senior priest vicars augmented his income for many years by keeping a small school in the Close. By virtue of his position, he had been collated to No. 14, the last house on the west side, which is much larger than the others, having an L-shaped wing adjoining the chapel. Another priest vicar reported that 'There were many old Books in the Library (above the chapel) till Mr Fosters School Boys were sufferd to throw them about & demolish them'. There is no indication that there was any way from No. 14 into the library direct, so the boys would have had to go round and through the chapel entrance, but Foster might well have been using the library as a school room. Some of the old books referred to may have been those of Dean Ralph Bathurst, bequeathed to the college in 1704. The books were removed from the library in about 1838 to preserve them from neglect and stored in the hall.[15]

The composer, John Broderip, had been organist and master of the choristers for thirty years when he died in 1771, and he was followed by two short-serving organists. Peter Parfitt was appointed his successor and admitted as a vicar. It is not clear where he had worked previously, but his unruly brother James had been a vicar since 1757. At the audit meeting in 1773, James had grossly insulted the principals and others and refused to apologise. The meeting voted to expel him and the steward, writing the minutes, said he thought him insane. He may have been drunk, but when he came to his senses, he apologised for his errors and was re-instated; he was finally expelled permanently in 1784.[16] Only one partial composition by Peter survives, insufficient to judge its quality, but he served only for two years before resigning his post, though he continued to retain his vicarship until his death in 1780 and there is a memorial slab to him in the nave of the cathedral. His successor, Robert Parry, held the post until 1781; beyond that, little or nothing is known of him. The next two organists, Dodd Perkins and his son William each served for 39 years. Dodd's skill as an organist appears to have been greater than his singing voice. When he was appointed in July 1781, his automatic election as a vicar was queried by Aaron Foster, who could not give his approval as to Dodd's voice and singing skills. He was admitted on a majority decision, but presumably improved during his probationary year because Foster registered no dissent at the time of his perpetuation; perhaps he had given him singing lessons, or perhaps Dodd's skill at teaching was sufficient to outweigh deficiencies in his vocal performance. No sacred music of his composition survives, but several secular songs are extant. During his time as master of the choristers, Wells had a chorister called Thomas Welsh, possibly the son of vicar John Welsh. Thomas has been described as 'the most remarkable boy soprano of the [18th] century'. While at Wells, visitors flocked to hear him and then Thomas Linley, the Bath composer and impresario, took him to London when the Theatre Royal, Drury Lane opened. Thomas made his debut in 1794 and for the next three years, until his voice broke, most operas staged at the theatre were designed 'to show off his remarkable high coloratura'[17]

In 1792 a disagreement with the Chapter, which had been rumbling on for a number of years, finally forced the college into a decision. In that year the hall meeting formally noted that since 1780, the Dean and Chapter had discontinued any *ex gratia* payments that they had been in the custom of making to the vicars choral, which the current vicars believed was payable to them from the rents and fines of escheatery lands, together with stall wages and other accustomed fees and dues.[18] All the Chapter Acts record is that in April 1780, the vicars were ordered to all attend the next meeting of Chapter, bringing with them their 1348 letters patent constituting them a corporate body. On 1 May, the greater part of their body attended and alleged they did not regard themselves obliged by law to produce their letters patent to Chapter. Chapter responded by decreeing that in future they would not therefore be paid any fees or perquisites for so contemptuously refusing to produce their letters patent. What the background to this was is not revealed, nor indeed, why the vicars waited for twelve years to do anything about it. The meeting in 1792 then appointed a committee of three of their number to examine all the records and papers relevant to their business deposited in the Tower of London and other places, that is, the records of government and the law courts. This was a formidable task by any measure and the meeting agreed to cover all the costs. The assumption is that they had already made a close study of their own records; it would be interesting to know whether they were granted access to Chapter records.[19] What happened thereafter, like the outcome of so many legal issues, is not recorded.

The comfortable, customary way of life of the eighteenth century continued well into the next. When the nineteenth century opened, Dodd Perkins had already been organist and master of the choristers for almost twenty years and he was to continue for another twenty, until his death in 1820. Two of Dodd's sons served as choristers, and in 1804 William was admitted as a vicar. Shortly after his father's death he was appointed to fill the vacant post. Like his father, he served as organist and master of the choristers for thirty-nine years; between them, therefore, the two Perkins controlled the musical life of Wells for almost eighty years, though not always satisfactorily. How often the choir rehearsed, if it did so at all, is not recorded, but in other cathedrals it was rarely.[20]

By the 1830s the winds of change that had begun to blow through the cathedrals were making themselves felt in Wells. The common perception of cathedrals in the first quarter of the century, both now and at the time, was that the cathedral canons were extremely wealthy, nepotistic, spiritually moribund and neglectful of both the needs of their glorious buildings and the poverty that surrounded them. Certainly they were rarely seen at services; these were very largely conducted by priest vicars, but even they often held other appointments and did not always fulfill their duties of conducting the services or of augmenting the choir.[21] Examples of all these things can certainly be found, but they are not necessarily the whole story. Many canons were considerable scholars and devoted time and money to charity and we have seen at Wells that the cathedral building was not wholly without care and attention. Likewise, if some of the vicars were lackadaisical about performing their duties, others served both the college and cathedral diligently and did their best, within limited means, to maintain their ancient college buildings. The growing pressure for reform in both Church and State led to a series of measures culminating in the Cathedrals Act of 1840. In broad terms, the staff and endowments were reduced and those who manned the cathedrals had perforce to become much more diligent in performing their duties. The changes were gradual, but over the next forty years or so life in the cathedral changed substantially.

CHAPTER SIX
REFORM AND REVIVAL

The reforming Act of 1840 changed the whole basis of cathedral finance by transferring all canonical and capitular estates to the Ecclesiastical Commission in exchange for fixed annual sums. It also had the effect of reducing the number of residentiary canons to four at all cathedrals (with the exceptions of Canterbury, Durham and Ely, six each, and Winchester, five) from a total that had varied at Wells from six to eight, including the dean. This took some time to come fully into effect as the canonries gradually fell vacant. The old custom at Wells for a newly appointed residentiary canon not to take up his place in the year he was elected or for a full year following, during which time any dividends to which he might have been entitled were divided among his fellow canons, was now abolished. The annual period of residence was fixed at eight months for the dean and three months for canons. All the money saved was henceforth to be poured into parish life, particularly in the growing towns and cities of Victorian England. The new residency rules also had the effect of discouraging plurality among senior clergymen, though many canons retained a parish. Just how effective the new rules on residency were is not clear, but the decline in numbers of canons available certainly made an impact on those vicars choral who were priests and who were expected to take up the slack, although in practice they had probably been doing so for years.[1] Having surrendered their prebendal estates to the Ecclesiastical Commissioners, at Wells, as elsewhere, the dean and residentiaries received fixed salaries in return: £1,000 p.a. for the dean and £500 p.a. for each canon. Non-residentiary prebendaries were likewise dis-endowed and their prebends transferred to the Commissioners, but they received nothing in return. The pace at which the surrender of all the capitular estates took place varied from cathedral to cathedral; in Wells the transfer happened in 1866.[2]

In 1852 the first of two Royal Commissions on cathedrals was appointed. It did not result in any specific legislation, but its report, based on questionaires sent to all the cathedrals, contains a wealth of material and gives a snapshot of life for the vicars of Wells as the reforms of 1840 began to take effect. In May 1853 the college received a letter from the Commissioners asking for copies of their deeds of foundation and endowment and particulars of the property currently belonging to it and statements of the gross and net income for the past seven years. The college minutes noted that while they were happy to provide such information, there were considerable cost implications which the vicars could not afford and which would have to be paid by the Commissioners.[3] The resulting Report showed that at Wells there were four priest vicars (or minor canons) and seven lay vicars, fewer than the charter of Queen Elizabeth permitted, which was a total of fourteen. The 1840 Act limited the number of minor canons or priest vicars at most cathedrals to between two and six. All the vicars were still nominated by the Dean and Chapter but had to be approved by members of the college as had been the practice for centuries. They generally lived in Wells, but not necessarily in the Close. There were morning and evening services every day, all of which were choral. All the vicars were required to be present at the Saturday morning service and both services on Sunday, and half the lay vicars were required alternately to attend all the others. The priest vicars were required during one week in four to take the services on Sunday as well as all the weekday ones. In return for holding almost all the services, priest vicars in every cathedral were to receive a salary of £150 p.a. The Report reflects the long-standing custom that none of the canons took any services at all, although special feast days were not mentioned in this context. Holy Communion was celebrated on the first Sunday of the month and at all great festivals. Sermons were preached at both Sunday services and at the morning service on holy days. These were the responsibility of the canons, but even then, the priest vicars sometimes ended up preaching in their place, but at least on those occasions they received an extra payment of two guineas. In 1856 Chapter agreed that vicars who attended services (and presumably sang in the choir) when it was their week off, would receive an extra payment of 1s.6d. per service.

The Report also printed the annual accounts of cathedral chapters for the years 1846-1852. In Wells, the annual income varied from £5107 to £4389, of which the portion paid to the vicars in total varied from £164 to £231 (for details see Appendix 3). In brief, cathedral funds only paid part of what was, for the vicars, less than a living wage. A far cry from the time in the Middle Ages, when each canon paid his own vicar about a quarter of his own income. The new regular salary for the priest vicars therefore was a ground-breaking step, taking them back to just over a quarter of a canon's salary. The remainder of the vicars' annual income came from the irregular payments from their own college estates and from whatever outside work they could take individually. To be fair to the Dean and Chapter, they had no detailed knowledge of the accounts of the college, since the latter jealously guarded its independence, and therefore they did not know what the vicars' actual incomes were, though they were aware of their inadequacy. Their sense of independence had not really worked to the advantage of the vicars. Their scattered estates were inefficient to administer and they were unable to institute new and progressive methods of land management. They did not, for instance, take advantage of rising land values and agricultural prosperity to raise rents, though they did increase the fines levied on lease renewals. To take only one example, the mill at Cheddar, which had continued to operate over the centuries, brought in the same rent in 1870 as it had in 1463 when Bishop Bekynton gave it to the college. Since the foundation of the college, the day-to-day estate management had been in the hands of the part-time reeve or bailiff of each estate or parcel of small estates, but the accounts were always formally audited and all new leases were approved by the vicars at hall meetings. The first college minute book begins in 1801, and one of the earliest entries noted that at Kingstone the chancel of the church was in such a bad state of repair that it was considered dangerous to go near it. There is, however, no indication that any decision was made to repair it. Later minutes show 'the Body', as the Hall meeting of the vicars referred to itself, considering requests to add lives to leases, the appointment of reeves, the sale of timber and often charging one of the principals to ride out and make enquiries. To that extent, the vicars took their land ownership seriously, and their Hall meetings were concerned almost exclusively with their properties in the early decades of the 19th cent., but they were completely unable to take any decisions that were not short-term. The college had only begun to employ a professional steward in the late 18th century, but how far that improved matters is open to question; for instance, at no point were accurate plans of their properties ever commissioned.[4]

To suppose that the college properties in Wells itself had been better administered, since they brought in the greater part of the vicars' income and were under their very noses, would be an error. All the leases had a requirement for the tenants to maintain the property during the lifetime of the lease, but there is no evidence that fines for lack of such repairs, or orders for them to be carried out were ever enforced. In the 1860s the Christopher Inn, the vicars' single most valuable property in the town, was in such a bad state of repair that it was uninhabitable. The Vicars Close houses were no better. Each vicar was collated to two houses on his appointment, an arrangement which dated back to the post-Reformation period. In theory this allowed him to live in one and supplement his income by letting the other. Since many of the vicars were married with families, the most practical solution was to amalgamate the two to form one reasonable sized dwelling house. Almost none of the vicars could afford to do this, so for the most part, they rented out both houses and found somewhere else to live themselves, leaving only single men in the Close. The 1851 census shows only three vicars living there. Naturally, none of the properties were properly maintained, since the individual vicars could not afford to do so. Nonetheless, it still mattered to the vicars which house they were collated to, either to occupy or collect rent from, since those houses which had been amalgamated brought in a much higher rent.

If the vicars had chosen to co-operate with Chapter, perhaps allowing their estates to be administered together with the cathedral ones in return for annual payments, they would certainly have been better off. In July 1852 they approached the Ecclesiastical Commissioners about the possibility of handing over the estates to them in return for such income 'as may upon examination appear just and fair'. The Commissioners refused on the grounds that College of Vicars Choral were not among the ecclesiastical corporations that the Acts regulating the Commissioners' proceedings enabled them to administer. In March 1864, owing to the 'indefatigable exertions' of the then principal, Mr Fletcher, the Commissioners were persuaded to hand over £24, being 6 years arrears on two suppressed canonries, which was immediately divided up among the vicars. In 1866 negotiations were re-opened with the Commissioners when they formally took over the capitular estates. This time agreement was reached and the Commissioners assumed responsibility for the college estates, paying an annual sum of £880 to the college; this was the sum offered by the Commissioners and the vicars failed to negotiate a larger one. In a financial statement, probably made as part of the negotiations, the vicars declared that in the ten years to December 1861, they had received a total of £5,678.6s.0d. from fines and heriots in addition to the regular rents. While annual returns fluctuated, this gives an annual average income of £567 16s. 0d., so in fact the Commission's figure was a relatively generous one. The highest fine the vicars had received in the last few decades was in 1860 when £2000 was paid for the renewal of the Kingstone lease. These figures for fines, however, did not necessarily appear in the college accounts. Rents and heriots are regularly entered, but there is a strong suggestion that the fines, when they accrued, were shared among the vicars on a private basis. This is implied by the case of Samuel Foster in August 1844, when he left Wells to become a lay clerk at St George's Chapel, Windsor. Letters of the college steward, Edmund Davies, show that Foster's former colleagues refused to allow him a share of any of the fines accruing for 1844, but these fines are nowhere recorded in the college accounts. When Davies died in August 1863, the vicars expressed their 'unfeigned sorrow' at the loss of their long serving steward.[5]

Issues concerning the number of vicars, their low incomes, their attendance at services and dilapidation payments on vacating their houses were to be almost perpetual for most of the century. In May 1854 there was a dispute over a house made vacant by the death of a vicar. The college chose a lay vicar, Silas Fletcher, to occupy it; this was disputed by one of the priest vicars, the Revd. Mr Hawes, who felt that since the house had been held by priest vicars for the previous 70 years, he had a better claim on it. In fact the college had no say in the matter, since the bishop had sole power to collate, and he confirmed it to Fletcher. He also pointed out that it was the duty of the vicars principal to observe each year any failings in the vicars' houses and instruct them to carry out repairs. The same issue arose at a visitation the bishop made in 1859. The exact nature of the argument was over dilapidations that should have been paid for by a departing vicar or, if dead, his representatives. On the death of Mr Parfitt, the vicars collated Joseph Gleaves to his former house (which again they had no right to do) and Gleaves sued Parfitt's widow for the dilapidations while refusing to pay them himself on the house he had previously been occupying. A despairing Bishop Eden urged the vicars to come to some authoritative decision with legal force and then enforce regular repairs. The vicars resolved the immediate problem by ordering that 5 years' rent at £10 p.a. be recovered from Gleaves to cover the cost of repairs on the house he had been occupying before he was collated to Parfitt's. If he carried out the repairs, the sum would be remitted, if not, it would be taken from his share of the common fund. As far as the repairs on Parfitt's house were concerned, Gleaves started a common law action against the widowed Mrs Parfitt to recover the cost of dilapidations. She was forced to concede and paid up because she could not afford the legal costs to defend her case. His colleagues felt Gleaves had gone against all the spirit and statutes of the college and objected vigorously. Gleaves was judged 'contumacious' and downgraded from his position as a senior vicar. This did not stop Thomas Wicks from following his example when he started legal proceedings for dilapidations against Silas Fletcher; Fletcher, too, paid up, giving Wickes nearly £80. Fletcher pointed out that it was only because he and Mrs Parfitt were persons of modest means and therefore capable of paying, that the legal attacks were made.[6]

In 1868 the vicars came to a formal decision about dilapidations. They appointed a surveyor, Edmund Hippesley, to determine at the death of any vicar the dilapidations on his house, but they also resolved that the representatives of the deceased should not be made to pay the complete bill, but only 75% of it. Then in 1872 the college passed an act rescinding all previous statutes relating to dilapidations. It was designed to provide an effective means of repairing houses without recourse to law, to benefit the widows and children of vicars and settle disputes. By it, all dividends for a year after death, the *annus mortis*, should be paid to the representatives of the deceased vicar and this would cover the cost of repairs. Both Gleaves and Wicks voted against the act and at the following college elections were passed over for office, despite their seniority, for protesting against the act. The bishop was called in as Visitor to adjudicate. Bishop Lord Arthur Hervey ruled that the election, though strictly legal, should not have been used as a means of coercion against those of different views, and went away to study the act and its implications. He finally ruled that the recent act had not been approved by him as Visitor and deplored the fact that the legal precedent had been set that representatives could be sued. He thought that the recent Ecclesiastical Dilapidations Bill, which covered vicarages and parsonages, should be brought into force on the vicars' houses, but the vicars protested that their incomes and houses were so small in comparison with parsonages that this would not be equitable. In the end, Bishop Hervey ruled that in a previous dispute in 1826 his predecessor had directed that the revenues arising from other houses in the Close (that is, those not held directly by vicars) should be applied for the repair of all the houses and that these injunctions had not been repealed and therefore should be complied with because they were still binding. Any future arrangements made by the college had to be submitted to him for formal approval.[7]

Three years later, there was further dissension with the bishop when he collated Mr Wiseman to a house recently left vacant by the resignation of Mr Kearton and the vicars thought they should have been consulted. The bishop stood firmly on his ancient rights and in January 1879 he finally responded to the vicars' memorial about dilapidations. After careful consideration, he had some minor points of objections including the deduction of 25% from the *annus mortuis* payments for dilapidations. He requested the vicars to draft a new act, following as closely as possible the Ecclesiastical Dilapidation Act. To embody the provisions, a surveyor should be appointed, either for a term of years or when required, at fixed rates (both to be approved by himself). The surveyor was to assess need and supervise the work. On the death of any vicar, his house was to remain with his widow or representatives for one year. All monies to which he would have been entitled were to be received by the principals and used to pay the surveyor and for any work required, the surplus going to his widow. The survey was to take place one year from the time of death and the incoming vicar was to arrange for the work to take place under the supervision of the surveyor and payment was to be made from the money held for that purpose by the principals. If one year's money was not sufficient, the balance was to be paid by the deceased vicar's representatives to the new vicar, a debt recoverable by law. No further work was to take place within five years and if the house was vacated within that time, the outgoing vicar was not liable for any repairs. For any house left vacant other than by death, all money due to the vacating vicar was to be held by the principals until a new vicar was collated, when he would get vacant possession and an immediate survey would be held. The cost of repairs was to be covered by the outgoing vicar and if he could not cover all of it, then the incoming one would make it up. The bishop concluded by emphasising the importance of having all the buildings insured: £150 cover was agreed for a single house, £250 for a double. The Hall agreed to draw up such an act and did so, submitting it for approval, which was given in January 1881. Vicars were to be responsible for insuring their own houses and they had to produce the policies to prove that they had done so. Unfortunately the act did not cover the question of fittings, which gave rise to yet another dispute. When Mr Kearton resigned, the surveyor, Mr Hippesley, valued the fittings of his house at £30. Because of the delay in appointing his successor, the principal, Mr Beauchamp, advanced the sum to Kearton from college funds, but on his collation Mr Wiseman refused to refund him.[8]

Events in the 1850s illustrate other problems that the college faced: the number of vicars and their attendance to their duties. They were brought into focus by the death of one of the priest vicars, the Revd. Aaron Foster. In September 1853, the Hall meeting noted that more than three months had elapsed since his death and the Dean and Chapter had failed to appoint a new vicar, so according to their charter, the vicars therefore had a right to nominate their own candidate. They wrote to Chapter pointing this out, but said they would refrain from doing so provided Chapter did not increase the number of vicars to more than eleven and would do all in their power to assist the vicars to obtain 'an augmented and fixed stipend in lieu of their current inadequate and uncertain remuneration'. In reply, the Chapter expressed their thanks, acknowledged their lapse and assured the vicars they had no intention of appointing more than eleven vicars. They did, however, deem it expedient in this case to appoint a new lay vicar rather than a priest vicar. At the same time they wrote to all the priest vicars separately, acknowledging the latters' refusal to accept the proposed sums for discharging the duties of a priest vicar left vacant by Foster's death, and pointing out that they could not promise to support an application to the Ecclesiastical Commissioners for an increase in the stipends of current priest vicars.

In September 1867 some of the vicars applied to Chapter for an increase in the payments for attendance at extra services. This had been set at 1s.6d. in 1856 for each service a vicar attended on his off-duty week. Now the vicars were asking for 2s.6d. As a result, Chapter asked their clerk to obtain details of similar payments at other cathedrals. He reported that he had obtained details from his colleagues at Bristol, Gloucester, Hereford, Salisbury and Worcester. The surprising result was that the vicars choral at Wells worked less and were paid more than any of their fellows. Since they were only required to attend services every other week, that worked out at three and a half days per week, for which they received £96 p.a. At the other end of the scale, the six lay clerks at Hereford sang two services daily and three on saints' days and were paid £61 p.a. At Wells, stall wages and gratuities from earlier benefactors added up to about an additional £3 p.a. and if a vicar chose to avail himself of the existing payment of 1s.6d. for extra services he could earn another £25 p.a. So no, there would be no increase to 2s.6d. In January 1870 Chapter took the decision that because the irregularity of attendance of many of the vicars was so great that 'much public comment' had been uttered and that it 'threw some discredit on the discipline of the Establishment', it was resolved to rescind the 1856 resolution on extra attendance payments and select only four vicars to receive the increased payment each quarter. And it would be made clear to vicars that any attendance at extra services would be set off against absences in duty weeks. The Chapter clerk was to monitor attendance and pay accordingly.[9]

In July 1874 the Dean and Chapter complained formally to the college about the non-attendance at services of certain members. It may seem strange to a modern reader that many vicars should have been so very lax in attending to the duties for which they were paid; the only explanations seem to be that their remuneration was meagre and they were secure in the knowledge that their appointment was for life. The Hall meeting that followed the complaint in 1874 resolved that each vicar was to fulfil his duties and attend every service during his duty week unless he was ill and if so, must formally notify Chapter. Two of the worst offenders at this period were Messrs Gleaves and Drayton. In 1860 when William Drayton was appointed there was clearly some question about his health because he was asked to produce a medical certificate at his interview, and there was a reference to his 'peculiar position', alas not specified; it can only be assumed that he had an exceptionally good voice. Over the next decade there are references to his repeated absences and what seems to have angered Chapter most was that he never explained them or made any apologies for them. If he was in Bath under doctors' orders, why could he not just write and explain and ask formally for sick leave? Drayton claimed that Chapter knew his health was so poor he was forced to give up singing and leave Wells for a period. He was under constant medical care and would undergo any medical examination Chapter wished. Chapter informed the college that unless Drayton fulfilled his duties or paid for a substitute, he would be replaced. Since it received no reply or apology, it suspended all payments to him and advertised for a bass to replace him. On the other hand, when Joseph Gleaves pleaded that illness was responsible for his several absences, he was told that his fines would not be remitted because his illness was not serious enough. In October 1873 Chapter settled the matter by sacking him for misconduct and uselessness as a singer, appointing John Wiseman as a substitute, but not a replacement, at £70 p.a. The college refused to accept Wiseman's nomination and in December 1874 it told Chapter that Gleaves had been absent for a year and the college would write to him requiring him to be back in his place by January. Chapter expressed surprise that the vicars had undertaken this step with regard to Gleaves while ignoring Drayton's continued absence without formal leave and failure to supply a substitute. In fact, Drayton seems to have been in Wells, acting as college principal and conducting business with Chapter. Clearly there was something wrong with his voice which prevented him singing. He was therefore served with a formal summons to attend a Chapter meeting and answer for his conduct in public. If he did not satisfactorily answer the charges, then he would be expelled. In the end, Drayton attended and submitted, agreeing to make a formal application for absence on the grounds of ill-health and pay half the salary of a substitute for the previous six months and for however long his absence continued. In April 1887 the canon in residence reported that a dispute between vicars Drayton and Merriman had led to a failure of duty at some services and the matter was referred to the vicar principals to effect a reconciliation. When their attempt failed, the whole matter was referred to the bishop as Visitor. As late as May 1892 Drayton wrote to the Chapter saying that because of an 'affliction of the chest' he would be unable to attend to his duties in the winter months and suggesting that instead of singing alternate weeks throughout the year he sing every week from April to October and take the rest of the year off. The Chapter could not agree to that, but it did tell him that if it proved necessary, and they hoped it would not, then they were prepared to consider other arrangements.

Joseph Gleaves continued to cause trouble. By September 1875 he had been absent from services on health grounds for well over a year and the college reluctantly agreed to withhold any payments due to him as a vicar and take steps to expel him. In the following month one of the vicars, Mr Kearton, complained that Gleaves had assaulted him over a borrowed surplice in the vicars' vestry in the cathedral, so the threat of expulsion had clearly had an effect and Gleaves was back at work. In the following January Gleaves petitioned the bishop over the with-holding of his share of monies, but rather than allow new proceedings before the bishop, the vicars caved in, agreed to rescind their decision and paid him. The main reason for this was the college's current dispute with the Dean and Chapter.[10]

In March 1875 Chapter had taken the step of submitting a case about the vicars to Dr Stephens, QC, essentially to discover if it had the power to increase the number of vicars to fourteen, while recognising that it would have to compensate existing vicars for their smaller dividends, and also whether it had the power to expel vicars; it had taken the precaution of ordering a copy of the vicars' 1591 charter from the Public Record Office. The legal answer to both questions was yes. Given the vicars' relatively poor record of attendance it is difficult not to feel some sympathy for Chapter. Unsurprisingly, the college thought that such a move would be entirely in Chapter's favour and took counsel's opinion itself. The Dean and Chapter had nominated John Wiseman to an existing vacancy, but for the time being, at least, the vicars refused to accept the nomination which they held was their right, and declined to administer the college oath. Battle was joined and the dean asked to see a copy of the statutes relating to the oath and submitted the case to his legal counsel. In September the bishop held a visitation as a result of petitions from the Dean and Chapter and from Wiseman, who had been left in limbo. Behind the scenes, frantic negotiations were going on, with the result that in October 1875 at a formal hearing held with both parties and their lawyers before the bishop, it was concluded that the numbers of vicars would be increased to fourteen on the basis of an arrangement agreed between the parties over the compensation paid to existing vicars and out of courtesy, the vicars offered the nomination of 3 new vicars to Chapter; this right, of course, already belonged to the latter. It was not, however, until a year later that three new vicars, including Wiseman, an alto, were admitted for their probationary year. Thereafter, those vicars who were in post in 1875 had different conditions of service to those appointed from that date. In 1883 both college and Chapter were forced to seek the bishop's judgement on interpretation of the terms of the arrangement about compensation. The bishop took advice from no less an authority than the Lord Chancellor. He found that the Chapter were only required to compensate those vicars in post in 1875, that was, to ensure that each man's share of the £880 paid to the college by the Ecclesiastical Commissioners did not fall below £80 by reason of there being an increase of the number of vicars from eleven to fourteen.[11]

The new arrangements of 1875 were too late to help with another crisis. In September 1876, the Dean and Chapter recorded their dissatisfaction (to say the least) that on the previous Sunday all three priest vicars were absent and only Dr Wallis had leave to be away and he had not bothered to arrange a substitute. It was apparently only by a fortunate accident that there was a visiting clergyman available to take the services. This incident led to the issuing of Rules and Regulations to be observed by all vicars. There was nothing new in them, but their codification was intended to leave the vicars in no doubt about their obligations and no excuses if they failed to observe them. Briefly they covered attendance at services and at the quarterly roll call in the Chapter House, namely, any absences to have received permission in writing from the Dean and Chapter and those with medical reasons to have submitted a medical certificate, the need to enter and leave services in procession, with any indecorous and irreverent behaviour during them to be considered a breach of duty, and finally if any vicar was unable to discharge their musical duties through age, illness or failure of voice, then if the Dean and Chapter so ordered, he was to pay one third of the salary of any substitute appointed to take his place. That the vicars did not already abide by such basic long-standing obligations may seem surprising, but clearly the Dean and Chapter had been fairly long-suffering over the issue. Despite new Rules and Regulations, in October 1888 instructions sent out to all persons applying to be lay vicars included the warning that all those who offended against the rules forming part of their contract with the Dean and Chapter either by neglect of duty or other misconduct were liable to be fined between £1 - £3 after due enquiry and opportunity for defence.[12]

Throughout the century, Chapter proved mindful from time to time of the vicars' financial difficulties. At Christmas 1848 they gave a gratuity of £20 to be divided between the six lay vicars because the receipts of the vicars choral had been 'very considerably diminished and inadequate to their necessary expenditure'. They were not, however, about to raise stipends on a permanent basis. One reason was the effect of the vicars' lifetime tenure of their office, so that even the very elderly or the sick retained their income. If their inability to attend to their duties was long-term, the Chapter was obliged to find and pay a deputy and hope that they could recover some portion of it from the vicar concerned. In 1836 an extra vicar, Mr Jerrard, was appointed to replace Mr Ball, who had been attending services on behalf of Mr Rolle, and in the same period, Chapter more than once gave donations of five guineas to vicars suffering from the expenses of long and severe illnesses. When, in April 1850, Mr Beauchamp returned to his duties after a lengthy absence, Chapter pointed out that it had paid for his share of the deputy's salary, and they now needed him to come to some form of arrangement so that he refunded £10 of it. The whole issue was compounded by the position of the organist and master of the choristers, for which see below.[13]

In response to a questionnaire sent them in May 1867 by the Ecclesiastical Commissioners about the income of the lay vicars, the college replied that there were eight of them, whose duties were to attend daily services, but there were no means of enforcing attendance. Their average income over the last 14 years had been £81 p.a., now paid by the Commissioners. They had no pensions. In addition they received £2 p.a. each, and the six seniors an additional £2 (£4 in all) in lieu of stall wages from the prebendaries. The Dean and Chapter paid each vicar £1 5s. 9d. per quarter as a stipend and a £10 pension from the Crown was divided equally among them. The vicars pointed out that the payments from the Dean and Chapter were still the same as when the income of the dean was £100 and the canons £20 p.a. (they were now £1,000 and £500 respectively). They ended their response by begging for a pension and declaring that they considered the income they received inadequate for the services they performed. In 1868 the college entered a long discussion with the Commission for Woods and Forests over the centuries-old payment of the £10 'Crown pension'. This came out of a sum of £58 9s. 3d. paid to the Dean and Chapter and they were currently failing to receive it. The Commission confirmed that the whole sum was now paid to the Ecclesiastical Commissioners, who in turn replied that the vicars' £10 was included in the commutation sum of £880 p.a. Yet again the vicars lost out.[14]

While the properties in Vicars Close were for the most part becoming slowly more dilapidated, they were beginning to attract the attention of serious antiquarians, whose interest in medieval architecture was above and beyond that of the 'gothick' style, fashionable in the late 18th century. John Carter, an artist and draughtsman, was commissioned by the Society of Antiquaries to make drawings of different cathedrals and came to Wells in the 1790s. His drawings of the hall and close were in many ways incidental to those of the cathedral, and unlike them, were not published at the time.[15] Carter was followed in the early 1800s by a number of antiquarian artists, of whom John Buckler's work is the most informative. More importantly, in 1832 Augustus Pugin and his son and namesake arrived in Wells and made a study of the best of the surviving medieval buildings. They produced detailed plans and cross-sections of the principle structures as well as details of various mouldings and other features. These were not, however, a study of the buildings as they appeared in 1832, but an interpretation, since they excluded anything they considered not to be a part of the original medieval buildings. It would probably not be going too far to say that the Close and the drawings of it the two Pugins made and published, had a considerable influence on the Gothic Revival movement.

Their work certainly inspired an Oxford architect called John Henry Parker, who came from a wealthy publishing family. Arriving in Wells in 1860, he purchased the interest of Edmund Davies, the college steward, in a lease of both the east end of the Hall and several of the houses (nos. 22, 27 and 28) and began a major restoration project. In the hall block, having obtained a lease on the kitchen for £10 in 1863, he extended the kitchen offices to the west and raised the roofline, inserting an oriel window copied from an original in No.1 St Andrew's Street. Parker was also permitted to erect a small gate to the west of the main gateway provided it caused no obstruction. Under the Hall itself, the cellar and storage space, where there is still evidence of some thirteenth century features of the original ground floor hall that preceded it, was modified to make it a usable space. It is currently the Chapter Room and consists of four bays, with a large fireplace and an ornate ceiling added by Parker. He employed William Burges to design suitable furniture (his Gothic dresser is now on the Chain Bridge) and Burges was responsible for the painted ceilings and for decoration in No. 22, where Parker lived for a while. The latter's photographs of the Close c.1865, issued as a supplement to his book on Wells, while not the earliest images of the Close by any means, are the first comprehensive study. In 1866 Parker applied for a lease of the whole hall in addition to his present holding and was refused. It was an unsatisfactory position for Parker but presumably the vicars wanted to retain a small part of the hall for their own use. He immediately came back with a proposal for a 21-year lease of the Hall with all its offices, the chapel and its library. He would carry out much-needed repair work and would under-let to the vicars those parts they required; it would naturally mean a reduction in rent. The proposal was refused, not least because the vicars 'consider the silliness and ignorance of Mr Parker's printed attack upon the College is only equalled by its impertinence'. Parker was given notice to quit the kitchen in July 1869 but in September 1870 the vicars finally gave in and granted him a lease for all the premises he had formerly held only under Edmund Davies' lease.[16]

Wells Theological College, which was founded in 1840 and one of the first of its kind, started its life in the Close. At first, all the students lived in the Close until their numbers grew too great and they scattered to other lodgings. The Close chapel was used for the inaugural service of the Theological College, although because of its small size, formal services thereafter were in the cathedral Lady Chapel. In 1848 the College principal wrote to the vicars proposing to undertake the restoration of the chapel in return for its use for daily prayers for the students. The vicars agreed provided the plans and specifications were approved by them, and provided also that it did not imply any future right to use the chapel nor that responsibility to repair it rested on the principal or his successors. For reasons unspecified the scheme came to nothing, perhaps because the cost turned out to be more than the fledgling college could afford. When the Ecclesiastical Commissioners took over the college estates and property in 1870, this included the Close itself; responsibility for the latter was not given to the Dean and Chapter until 1980. This meant that henceforth all leases of property in the Close, save for the houses allocated to the vicars themselves for which the bishop retained the right of collation and were excepted from the scheme (the vicars were also permitted to retain the use of their Hall and offices, which seems to have included the chapel), were handled by the Commissioners. They were therefore responsible, probably at the request of the bishop, for continuing to lease accommodation in the Close to the Theological College.

Nearly thirty years later, in 1875, one of the Theological staff, horrified by the dilapidated condition of the chapel, obtained permission to launch a scheme for its restoration. By the following year it had been repaired and beautified at a cost of over £1000 and so too, had the room above, which, supplied with a new fireplace, could be used as a vestry or lecture room. In return the Theological College took over the chapel at a nominal rent of 1s. p.a. for fifty years. At this point, many services were held in the chapel of the Palace, which the bishop had made available in 1849 as a replacement for the use of the Lady Chapel. From the setting up of the College, the Dean and Chapter had made available part of their Library (the area at the north end, closest to the cathedral and quite separate from the chained library) for use as a lecture room, while the students used Vicars' Hall as their library. In 1860 it had been rented for £10 p.a. on the understanding that the vicars could have exclusive use of it whenever they had business to transact and gave the librarians notice the previous evening, and that their consent was obtained for any alterations to the hall and its fittings. In 1890 purchase of the Archdeacon's House (now the Cathedral School's Music Department) provided a large library space and lecture rooms after extensive restoration; Vicars Hall was deemed too cramped and too cold and draughty for the students. Gradually the trustees of the Theological College bought five properties in the Close from the Ecclesiastical Commissioners, as well as the canonical house (now the Museum) next to the Archdeacon's House and leased 'The Cedars' in the Liberty, while 'The Rib' provided accommodation for the college principal. The example set by the Theological College trustees in renting and restoring the ancient buildings did much to save the Close from decline and dereliction. Gradually modern life crept in; in 1852 the Paving and Lighting Commissioners agreed to repair the public gravel walk through the Close, though the vicars had to cover at least some of the cost, and in February 1856 it was agreed that the Wells Gas Light Company would supply gas to the Close.[17]

For the vicars choral themselves, estate, architectural and antiquarian matters were very much less important than their music and all was not well in the musical world of the cathedral in the early 19th century. William Perkins, who had succeeded his father, Dodd, as organist and master of the choristers in 1820, did not take his duties as seriously as the Chapter might have wished. In 1831, it ordered that the organist ' be spoken to, to have an Anthem every Wednesday and Friday. Three of William's anthem compositions survive, but can hardly be said to be of a very high standard. The Chapter was also of opinion that as 'his Apprentice was not equal to the Organ duty, it was expected of him to get a more efficient Assistant'. Following this instruction, Perkins appointed Alfred Angel, a former chorister, as his new apprentice; Angel went on to be organist at Exeter Cathedral, so was presumably of an acceptable standard at Wells. In 1832, Chapter again expressed dissatisfaction with the way Perkins fulfilled his obligations, this time with his teaching of the choristers. Many cathedrals had regular choir practices several times a week, and although it was ordered in 1831 that there be a full practice at Wells every Saturday morning, Perkins was reluctant to arrange rehearsals for the choristers.[18] He finally dealt with the problem by having Angel formally appointed under-master of the choristers in 1838, probably a job he had been doing for some time. In 1836 the old medieval choristers' house, known by this date as the Organist's House, which stood between the West Cloister and Penniless Porch, was damaged by fire. The Chapter proved willing to make good the damage on condition that Perkins take out in future an insurance policy with the Sun Fire Office. Later the house was in need of serious repairs to the roof which Chapter deemed

Perkins' responsibility, so they refused to pay for it and therefore nothing was done. It is not clear whether the choristers were still living in the house under the supervision of the assistant master at this point. In 1842, when Angel moved to Exeter Cathedral, he was replaced as assistant organist at Wells by another former chorister, Charles Lavington.[19]

Perkins himself seems to have spent much of his time living at the top of East Wells, an area known as 'Turkey', where he had bought a small farm. He was highly regarded by the locals, with whom he was very friendly. According to the memoirs of a local lady, Mrs E.M. Church, he was 'very free with them, and encouraged them all ways'. He was popular enough to get away with destroying the local bull-baiting ring in the year that he was mayor of 'Turkey'. Mrs Church does not say what year that was, or what duties the surely unofficial post of mayor involved. What he was not doing was fulfilling his obligations to the cathedral. Almost from the time of his appointment as Perkins' deputy in 1843, Charles Lavington apparently assumed all the older man's responsibilities for music in the cathedral. Lavington, born in 1819, had been a chorister at Wells and a pupil of Perkins before studying under James Turle, organist of Westminster Abbey. The Chapter were aware of how lucky they were to have him, making him several rewards on top of his salary for his 'able services and exemplary character'. In 1848 it was he and not Perkins who was asked to provide regular reports on the conduct and proficiency of the choristers. By 1850 the Chapter was complaining, not without cause, that Perkins continued to hold the offices of vicar choral and organist without discharging the duties of either. He was therefore ordered to provide a deputy for the choir out of his own salary. This was presumably not because Lavington was unpaid for the work, but that the Chapter was trying to get Perkins to take over such payment. This may have worked for a few years, but by 1859 Chapter had finally had enough. Perkins was an old and ailing man, completely unwilling or unable to perform the duties for which he was drawing his salary, and the Chapter clerk was asked to call on Mr Perkins and express the general wish that he should resign the post of organist.

Perkins was perfectly willing to comply and offer his resignation, but only if guaranteed an allowance of £50 p.a. for the remainder of his life. The Chapter refused. The crisis was resolved in July 1859 by a masterly piece of diplomacy. Perkins resigned on the understanding that any organist appointed during his lifetime would pay him £28 p.a. from his own salary. Charles Lavington was immediately elected organist and master of the choristers and the Chapter agreed to pay him an additional £20 p.a. salary as deputy organist during

Perkins' lifetime in addition to his salary as organist. This unusual arrangement lasted for just over a year. William Perkins died in November 1860 and was buried beside his father in the Palm Churchyard. Lavington complained about the dilapidated condition of the medieval organist's house; the Chapter tried and failed to obtain the cost of repairs from Perkins' executors and Lavington was allocated one of the canonical houses. By the 1860s the organist's house was clearly uninhabitable and Chapter were considering what to do about it. Various solutions were proposed: pull down the house and rebuilt a new one from the materials, or to pull down the more modern parts and repair the ancient parts sufficiently to save them from total decay. In 1869 the order was given to demolish the entire structure, though in fact part of the ancient walls were preserved and were still standing at the beginning of the twenty-first century, when they were incorporated into the staircase leading to the restaurant in the new Entry Cloister.[20]

Lavington, although a former chorister at Wells, was the first full organist not to be a vicar choral. There is no obvious explanation for this, but despite not formally being a member of the college, his occupation of the post affected the musical lives of all his colleagues. Like his two predecessors, he held office for a very long time, from 1859 to 1895. Unlike them, he seems to have been on good terms with the Chapter, which raised his salary to £150 following the death of William Perkins, partly at least to compensate for the fact that he did not also receive a vicar's income. In 1870 the Chapter gave him £5 to cover the costs of a journey to London to consult an oculist because of 'his serious imperfection of vision'. Immediately after his appointment to the post, he made it clear that the laxity of the previous regime would not continue under him by expelling two choristers, one of them for simply being absent on a Sunday. Several of his compositions survive in the part books and according to Barnes, although he could be guilty of the 'harmonic excesses' found in much Victorian music, he was also capable of 'expressive and effective writing'. More important, perhaps, was his attitude of 'devout reverence in all things connected with the services of the Church', both in the cathedral and in the Close chapel for the theological students. Many years after his death, a tribute to him says 'It was impossible to spend an hour in his presence without feeling that here indeed was a "holy and humble man of heart".[21] Several major developments took place during Lavington's tenure. First was the use of printed music, which during the 1840s and 1850s was revolutionised by Novello's publishing house and thus became affordable for cathedral choirs. Cheap printed music replaced the manuscript part-books, which contained much music written in Wells and into which one printed sheet of new compositions from elsewhere had been easily and cheaply copied to save expense. Being able to afford multiple printed copies meant the much wider use of the great Victorian composers of church music, and the gradual exclusion of any earlier Wells material. The second development was the rebuilding of the cathedral organ in 1857 by Henry Willis, originally intended to be just a modification of the 1786 Green organ, but finally giving the cathedral an organ worthy of the finest church music.

Another development affected the choristers rather than the vicars. Their school, officially the cathedral grammar school, situated since the Middle Ages in the purpose-built hall above the West Cloister, and taking in selected boys from the town as well, had fluctuated in standard depending entirely on the quality of the master appointed to teach them. In the first quarter of the 19th century, there were several who were scholars, but thereafter the school went into decline. In 1870 Chapter finally decided to close it and came to an arrangement with the Revd. Mr Palmer, master of Wells Middle School, to take the twelve choristers at a cost of £12.50 per quarter. The exact hours of their tuition was to be arranged with Lavington and they were to be escorted to and fro by a trustworthy person. In 1879 Mr Palmer applied for an increase in his payment and thereafter received £60 p.a. Two months later Chapter applied to the Ecclesiastical Commissioners for funding to establish a grammar school in Wells; their application was turned down. In June 1880 it was considering the possibility of turning the house that now houses Wells Museum into a school. It was occupied by Mr Elwes, the vice-principal of the Theological College, but the likely cost of repairs led to the decision not to purchase. In December 1880 the matter was resolved. Mr Abram, who had purchased the good will of a school previously carried on by Robert Young, became the tenant of Mr Elwes' house and opened a school there. Chapter decided to entrust the education of the choristers to Mr Abram and remunerate him at £100 p.a. This is the school that subsequently became the Cathedral School. In March 1900 the father of one of the choristers named Davies 'brought forward' a matter concerning the assistant master, a priest vicar named Henry Leigh Lye, who treated the boarders in the School House 'with imprudence and a lack of delicacy'. After a full enquiry Leigh Lye was reprimanded, but a more serious charge was deferred until the return of the chorister, who had left, to give evidence. The reprimand seems to have had little effect, because a year later, despite the repeated instructions given to him after further complaints from the choristers, the Chapter resolved to suspend Leigh Lye from his connection with the Grammar School. His response was immediately to resign his mastership and from his post as priest vicar. Victorian susceptibility means exactly what his offences were remained unspecified, though they may well have been less than the conclusion to which a twenty-first century mind immediately leaps.[22]

Charles Lavington died in 1895. He had been ill for a year before that and had been assisted by C.H. Moody, who was also the bishop's private organist and went on to be organist of Ripon Cathedral. Shortly before Lavington's death the Chapter agreed that a new priest vicar, Thomas Davies, should take over in the interim. In 1896 Dr Percy Buck was formally appointed organist. The following year, when a vacancy occurred for Diocesan Choir Master, Chapter felt that it was very likely that Buck would be approached; the precentor felt that with safeguards, it would be possible for him to do both jobs. Buck was clearly highly valued by Chapter, which, on learning that he was considering taking up the vacant post at Bristol Cathedral, increased his salary by £50 to £250 p.a. This did not prevent him moving to Bristol in 1899; he subsequently went on to become Professor of Music at London University. When Buck left, Thomas Davies was formally appointed in his place. As well as being a priest vicar, he was one of the schoolmasters, and he gave up both these posts.[23]

In October 1898, three of the vicars asked for the time of Evensong to be fixed at 3.00 p.m. throughout the year, to enable them to get to neighbouring towns where they had employment (evening tuition, bar work?). Chapter took their request seriously and decided to ask Dr Buck and the three schoolmasters if not 3.00 but 3.30 p.m., would be a convenient time for them. Eighteen months later it was reported that a 3.30 p.m. start time was preferred by most vicars. For some reason, presumably opposition by some of its members, Chapter did not find this acceptable. However, the Precentor proposed a compromise. If the start time was to be 4.00 p.m., during the winter months the vicars should have two days off per week, and he submitted a draft agreement to be signed by all new vicars that if this favour was granted them, they would promise to ensure that there would always be six men present on weekdays and eight on Wednesdays. It was decided to try this arrangement as an experiment. This led on to the question of choir holidays in the summer. In 1899 the organist, Dr Buck, proposed that they be fixed for the first half of August so that all the boys could get away at the same time, with half the vicars off in late July and the other half in early August. Instead, Chapter agreed that the services should be said and not sung for thirteen days from Monday 31 July.[24]

In general, the Dean and Chapter took seriously their responsibility for the recruitment of the vicars choral. In 1865, following the death of the Revd. Du Cane, two of the remaining priest vicars were paid an additional £3 per week as they took on responsibility for his share of the services. In October there were several candidates for the vacant post. Some were excluded because they held a preferment at a distance from Wells, and two were called to interview with the Dean and asked to take a service. Three years later, on the death of Mr Burr, the senior lay vicar, an advert was placed in the *Musical Times* for ' a person aged from 25-30 with a high tenor voice, experienced in Cathedral Music and of good moral Character'. Payment was £60 p.a. for the probationary year. Mr Beauchamp, who had just succeeded Burr as senior lay vicar, was to receive the stall wages of Old Cleeve ((£2 10s. 8d. p.a.) as an addition to his stipend. It has been noted that it was not uncommon for a supernumerary vicar to be employed to cover for a sick or very elderly vicar. In 1872, Mr Greenwood, who had been filling such a temporary post and been paid £70 p.a. for this task, was told that it was not likely that he would be permanently recruited into the choir, 'his voice not being considered of sufficient compass', but when he got a job in Cambridge and prepared to leave, he was given a gratuity of £20 because of his exemplary conduct while at Wells.[25]

In light of the historical nature of some of the disagreements between the college and Chapter, it is worth noting that in 1881 the principal drew the vicars' attention to the state of their old records and documents and it was resolved that they should be inspected and properly preserved, and the Dean and Chapter agreed to pay half the cost of classifying and indexing them. In January 1882 Mr Birch was contracted to clean and list the documents for a sum of £12. A few years later, the Revd. Dr Wallis made an English translation of the 1591 charter and it was decided to print fifty copies so that new vicars could be given a copy to help them understand the historical background to their post. It was not, however, until 1901 that Mr Foster, the steward, handed over all the documents in his care to the vicar principal and the muniment room in the tower block put in order to receive them. In 1886 another historical point had arisen when the Chapter enquired whether the vicars claimed any interest in the Chain Gate. The answer was, yes, they did; it had not been individually specified when the Ecclesiastical Commissioners took over so had not been transferred to them. In which case, responded the Chapter, the 1459 licence granted to them by Bishop Bekynton bound the vicars to keep it in good repair and what were they going to do about the current much needed repairs? This was a bit of a poser, but the vicars replied that though they accepted that the licence meant the repairs were their responsibility, the present circumstances were so different that they did not feel legally bound to do the repairs. It was highly unlikely that the Chapter seriously expected the vicars to be able to furnish the money.[26]

Alongside the questions of absenteeism, the age-old problems of the vicars' behaviour did still arise, but over the course of the second half of the nineteenth century, complaints became much rarer. In June 1870 Mr Fletcher was suspended from his place in the choir by the Chapter for conduct which they regarded as a 'grave breach of moral propriety' (unfortunately unspecified – perhaps drunkenness in a public place). The senior priest vicar, Dr Wallis, pleaded on his behalf that he be allowed to withdraw voluntarily rather than be suspended and said he would put his apologies in writing to Chapter. Chapter reserved judgment until they received the latter, but it was not until six months later that Fletcher was permitted to resume his place in the choir, but not to take part in the services as a vicar choral, nor be paid for any extra attendances. In 1886 the Dean and Chapter received a memorial from the priest vicars calling their attention to the bad behaviour of some of the lay vicars during divine service, 'talking laughing, humming tunes and general irreverent behaviour'. The dean addressed the vicars on the subject in the Chapter House, but pointed out to the college that under their charter Chapter had the power to both make rules and deprive for ill-behaviour. In addition, under their contracts, vicars who offended by neglect of their duties or misconduct in church were liable to fines of between £1 and £3 by the Dean and Chapter after due enquiry. In October 1897 the vicars expressed to the Chapter their dissatisfaction with the home life of Arthur Taylor (another case where discretion means that the reason for the disquiet was not spelled out), but for some reason Chapter felt that it could not 'take notice' at present.

In August 1891 an unprecedented situation arose when William Merriman was declared bankrupt. Since he had been absent for more than 150 services and the college had already threatened him with expulsion, it was probably a relief to be able to report that he was absent from Wells and unlikely to return. He had promised the college he would resign voluntarily, though he now rescinded this; he had received part of a loan from the Dean and Chapter, which reluctantly agreed to pay the balance it had promised (£11. 5s.6d.), and at a meeting with the college principals it was agreed that if he did return to Wells, he would not be allowed to undertake any duties in the choir. The college again wrote formally to him requesting his resignation, with the undertaking that if they had to take the step of expelling him, the Chapter would fund any legal cost. In January 1892 the college expelled him, but the chancellor saw Merriman personally and told him that if he formally resigned, he would be paid to the end of 1891 with an additional sum of £10.

The bankruptcy court repaid part of the Chapter's loan, leaving a balance of £9 12s.4d. which it accepted as a bad debt. A few years later, when Chapter noted in 1899 that Fergus Asquith, one of the lay vicars, was making arrangements with his creditors, members unanimously felt that he was to blame for his predicament and nothing further could be done for him. It is worth noting that when the advertisement went out for a bass to replace Merriman, there were no fewer than 37 applicants. The position of a vicar choral may not have been very well paid, but it was for life, it was secure and it provided a job dedicated to music.[27]

CHAPTER SEVEN
CONTINUITY AND CHANGE

The college of vicars choral entered the 20th century expecting little change from the preceding decades. This was certainly borne out by the issues arising in the first few years of the new century. In 1900 the large south window in the hall needed restoration work which entailed a virtual rebuild and a few months later the 'square south chimney' cost £11 5s. to repair. In 1902 a proposal was agreed that the rent paid for the hall (it was then let for 21 years at a rent of £9 12s. p.a. to the Freemasons, on a lease that required them to undertake both internal and external repairs) should be set aside to form a fabric fund, but there was no chance of such a fund being built up before the south east window of the hall needed repair and the vicars had to contemplate the sale of the college silver to fund it. This suggests that they were incapable of enforcing the repair clause in the lease. In 1903 the Cathedral architect, Edmund Buckle, issued a report on the hall and staircase block, which showed that repairs costing £950 were urgently needed. The Chapter was unable to help because it had just spent a much larger sum on repairs in the cathedral and had no spare money. It suggested that the college hand over the hall, chapel and library to the Ecclesiastical Commissioners and get them to do the repairs and promised to support such an application. The college wrote to the Commissioners, declaring that the dilapidations were so serious that it was completely impossible for them to contemplate making the necessary outlay from their own resources. They enclosed a copy of the report and sought help for 'a group of ecclesiastical buildings unique in their antiquity, beauty and completeness'. The Chapter did indeed write in support, but told the Commissioners that the vicars had 'totally neglected' their buildings for many years until now they were in serious danger of collapse, for 'given ownership and time the vicars choral would let anything, merely ancient and beautiful, perish'. It was a harsh judgment, but not untrue.[1]

It is unclear exactly what the Commissioners' response was, but in their reply to it the vicars said their college had already incurred expense 'under pressure from the public' beyond their means to make part of the building safe and while thanking the Commissioners for their kind offer, they felt it utterly impossible to accept it owing to 'the impecuniosity of the body'. This suggests that the Commissioners had offered to make a substantial contribution but required a similar input from the college. The latter then appealed to the Dean and Chapter and applied to the bishop as well for approval to sell their silver.

Bishop Kennion was strongly against this and suggested an application to Queen Anne's Bounty for help. The college directed £25 p.a. into the fabric fund from 1906 for the next five years, the Dean and Chapter promised £50, and the college braced itself to borrow from the bank if funds proved insufficient. The first part of the restoration work specified in Buckle's report got under way; this was the repair of the tower block, since falling stones from there would threaten the safety of the residents of the Close, but meanwhile the Freemasons were complaining that wet was coming through the roof of the hall. In 1910 immediate repairs were needed to the east window at a cost of £65.[2]

Fortunately for the college, the fund-raising efforts seem to have been reasonably successful. In 1910 the Theological College's 21-year lease on numbers 10 Cathedral Green and 27 Vicars Close came to an end. It did not want another long lease on No. 10, but paid a fine of £115 for No. 27. Another body took a 3-year lease on No. 10 with a fine of £100. Both fines were paid into the fabric fund. Since these properties were in the hands of the Ecclesiastical Commissioners, it suggests that the latter offered the fines as their contribution to the repairs. A year later five of the vicars pledged £1 p.a. each for five years from their own income as well as their share of the common fund to the fabric fund. The new dean, Armitage Robinson, was so impressed by the efforts the vicars were making that he offered to contribute a sum personally. One effect of the repairs to the hall was the decision to move the historic picture of the vicars to a position where it was less likely to be affected by smoke and dust from the stove, though it took nearly three years for this to actually happen. In 1908 when the vicars' property was re-valued for insurance, the hall and tower block was valued at £1,250, with furniture and fittings at £100, but the picture at £200. No insurance value was placed on the archives, but in January 1912 the college was prepared to agree to the repair of the most valuable, particularly Bishop Bekynton's statutes. In December of the same year it was noted that the Wells Archaeological Society had purchased documents, some of which had once belonged to the vicars and they should attempt to buy them back. There was also approval for a plan to write a booklet about their hall, which would be for sale to the public, and that Mrs Fry, the caretaker, should show visitors around it and retain 20% of the income from it; the rest would go to the fabric fund.[3]

Occasionally it is possible to glimpse the standard of music at Wells before the era of widespread publicity. In June 1909, Bishop Kennion wrote to the vicars thanking them for their 'splendid contribution' to the Millenium

Celebrations for the cathedral. Two years earlier, the Dean and Chapter had expressed their concern about the efficiency of the choral services because of the age and infirmity of a number of the vicars, and felt they had to take measures to restore the previous 'high standard of music'. These worries seem to have related specifically to lay vicars because in 1894, Chapter had insisted that priest vicars have a clause in their contracts specifying that in the event of long-term incapacity they must resign, because with only three priest vicars to take the services, if any of them were seriously sick, the system would not work. The college could not object to this, since technically it did not affect the priest vicars' membership of the college. In 1906 Chapter received a letter from the vicars' steward saying the vicars principal could do nothing to compel William Drayton to provide a substitute; this was the start of a long and serious interchange between Chapter and college. In 1907, Chapter asked the college to consider the means and methods of providing substitutes for any vicar unable through age or infirmity to fulfil their duties. The latter batted the ball back by insisting that it wanted some firm proposals while promising cooperation. Chapter replied, having taken counsel's opinion, that it had the power to suspend and remove from office vicars no longer capable of discharging their duties and to issue rules and regulations for the future governance of the choir. While they were reluctant to exercise their full authority over long-serving vicars, they proposed that in six months time, after July 1907, they would suspend Drayton and Thomas Wicks, the two most senior members, and appoint substitutes. The cost would be partly covered by deducting from their payments a proportion of them not exceeding a third of the sum paid by the Chapter for their substitute, who would be paid £80 p.a. If the two did not sing in services, they might join in the processions and still have a seat in the Quire. Again, because it did not affect membership of the college, the latter did not object. Wicks and Drayton certainly did. Wicks demanded full payment for life, appearing with a lawyer at a meeting in the Chapter House, but the Chapter stood firm, declining to continue any part of their customary payment to him; he was not being removed from the college and therefore still had 'a handsome' income (a judgment most vicars would have disputed). In the end, Chapter suggested a compromise by which Wicks paid £25 p.a. towards the cost of his substitute; his lawyer offered £10, but in the end agreed to Chapter's terms. Drayton wanted to resign in return for an annuity of £92 10s. for life and a further 1 year for his widow. Chapter refused to budge and he finally accepted the same terms as Wicks. This was an issue which had dogged the choir for centuries and on this occasion seems to have been sensibly settled with the final agreement of all parties.[4]

The co-operative relations between the Dean and Chapter and the college was severely put to the test over the matter of vicar Arthur Taylor. In May 1907, at a formal meeting in the Chapter House, the college had made a presentment against Taylor for his failure to attend services and practices. Chapter ruled that he forfeit his right to any leave on Saturdays and in future he would be fined 2s.6d. for every service or practice missed. This led the college to resolve in 1912 that if a member missed a service he would be fined 2s.6d., which would be paid to the man who substituted for him, unless the latter was repaid in kind before the end of the current quarter. This suggests that the long custom of vicars being on duty one week in two still pertained. In May 1913 the Chapter was forced to write to the college, complaining about the inefficient way that Mr Taylor was performing the tenor part of the Cantoris side, particularly on Saturdays. They felt that if he could not perform better, the vicars needed to send another of their number to support him. In reply the college acknowledged the situation but reported that Mr Taylor was determined to improve and hoped that a second vicar would not be necessary. In January 1914 Mr Taylor was twice absent from his duties without finding a substitute and in addition had been rude to the Priest Principal. The Chancellor (presumably in the absence of the Precentor) had written to ask the vicars to deal with the matter. A hall meeting decided that since such behaviour inconvenienced his colleagues, each occasion should be dealt with by the principals on a day-to-day basis without further authority and they could fine him up to £1 per time. The vicars were therefore outraged in November 1915 when they received notice from the Dean and Chapter that they were removing Taylor from office for 'irregularity of attendance, inefficiency as a member of the choir and insubordination towards the organist'. Because of his poverty, they would charitably make him an allowance of 10s. per week until he became eligible for the recently introduced old age pension, and then they would reduce it to 5s.

The College saw such a move as an attack on its rights and were willing to resort to law if necessary to defend them, even if it meant selling their silver (valued at £2,000) to fund their legal defence, often their last ditch solution to raising funds but up to that date never put into practice. Several vicars said they had been induced to come to Wells because it was a lifetime appointment and that the organist (Thomas Davies, who had himself been a priest vicar from 1895 and was appointed organist in 1899) had given much provocation and had been warned about it by several of their number. The college maintained that it had the right of expulsion, but that Taylor had not been absent much recently, a tendency that had been cured by the fines it had imposed, a sanction also open to the Chapter. As for his inefficiency, he was 68 years old and if Chapter felt he could no longer perform satisfactorily, the customary procedure was for a deputy to be employed with the cost deducted from his salary, the system agreed by both the college and Chapter in 1909. The insubordination was a single incident, which the organist, knowing Taylor's fiery temper, could have handled more tactfully. Finally, if a pension was to be paid, the sum offered was an insult to the whole college. They all felt bound to defend the rights of their body and not have their charters and statutes treated as 'mere scraps of paper'. The Dean and Chapter countered by claiming that it had right and precedent over expulsion, but offered to withdraw it and expunge it from the record if the college itself expelled him; they would still give the money as a free gift. The college refused. What would have happened is anybody's guess, but luckily both parties were rescued from their entrenched positions by Taylor's timely death in February 1916; the Chapter granted his widow £10.[5]

The first mention of the European war does not appear in the vicars' own records until November 1915. This is not really surprising, given the age profile of almost all of them, but at that date a probationary vicar, David Appleyard, enquired as to whether, if he enlisted, his perpetuation would still take place when it was due. He was told that even if he did enlist, it was unlikely that he would be called up for military duties before the due date. This seems to have been what happened; a substitute for him was still in place in January 1917. A month after Apppleyard's enquiry, one of the priest vicars, the Revd. Hodgson, wrote to the Chapter asking for permission to enlist and making a proposal for the payment of the two remaining priest vicars who were willing to undertake his duties. Some of the Chapter felt that it was not consistent with his sacred office to enlist as a combatant, but it was eventually decided to agree to his terms if he did indeed enlist and was called for service.[6]

John Miller's health in August 1916 was giving the Chapter cause for serious concern in case he spread his infection to the boys or other vicars; he was suffering from pulmonary tuberculosis. In October 1916 the vicars asked the Dean and Chapter if they could provide a substitute for him; this suggestion was declined on the financial grounds that they had been paying for a number of substitutes for vicars no longer competent to perform while receiving no financial help from the vicars concerned, who continued to draw nearly their full income, including one on military service (Appleyard). The college felt it should seek legal advice on its position over the removal of vicars for inefficiency on the grounds of advancing age or infirmity, the role of the bishop as Visitor and whether the Dean and Chapter were bound to provide substitutes under the Rules and Regulations of 1876 regarding the vicars (see p. 91). Meanwhile, the Chapter clerk wrote to the college that with the vacancy caused by Taylor's death yet unfilled, Appleyard away and Miller unfit, the number of tenors was reduced to two and without undue strain on them, the college was unable to maintain the services in the accustomed manner. For November and December that year, the Chapter decided to have plain morning services and evensong only on Wednesdays.

In these circumstances, the Chapter felt compelled to remove members of the choir not fit to fulfil their duties. It proposed that William Drayton (appointed in 1860), whose life was drawing to a close, should suffer no financial loss, that John Miller should be granted a pension of £50 p.a., rising to £60 if it was impossible for him to retain his house. If the college would act immediately to remove Miller, the Chapter would put into immediate effect a pension scheme for existing lay vicars of £50/60. New members, including Appleyard, were to come under a new scheme to be considered by the vicars. Miller refused the terms on the grounds that he had no other form of income. The concept of pensions, though first introduced in the mid-nineteenth century, chiefly for military personnel, was by no means universal at the turn of the twentieth century; most people worked until they dropped because they had no alternative. The introduction of a state-funded old-age pension in 1912 by the Liberal government of Lloyd George changed all that. All employers had at least to consider, even if they rejected the idea, the payment of an occupational pension for long-serving employees, hence the Chapter's offer to the vicars. The college was very reluctant to force out an old colleague like Miller, partly because it had been legally advised that it had no power to do so, and partly because every organisation was suffering the loss of personnel due to the war and had to carry on short-handed. It did, however, persuade Miller to resign and give up his house and his post-mortem rights in return for a pension of £75 p.a. for life and a discharge for dilapidations on his house; it sounds as though some serious bargaining had gone on, but the college felt that if Chapter were able to accept this, then they might be able to persuade other vicars to resign. It appeared to them that this was the only practical solution since no scheme based on compulsory retirement would be acceptable. While the Dean and Chapter did not accept that the vicars lacked the power, under Chapter, to remove members of the college, they were willing to postpone the whole issue until after the war. It was not until early 1918 that Miller finally left.[7]

The hall had been let to the Freemasons since 1890 and they had renewed their lease as recently as 1912, but in 1917 they surrendered it and took one on No. 28 Vicars Close instead. This gave the college an opportunity to 'beautify' their hall. They proposed to remove the passageway through it, which had originally been made simply of canvas and then replaced by a lath and plaster one by the Freemasons, as well as the gallery at the west end. By returning the hall to what they regarded as its 'ancient condition', and displaying some of their valuable possessions, the vicars hoped to be able to increase the number of visitors who would pay to see it, thus helping to defray the cost of restoration. They also ordered a reprint of one thousand copies of the booklet about the hall, which were sold for 4d. each; no copy of this work seems to have survived. The restoration was postponed and eventually got under way in 1923. The college approached the bishop about a public appeal to help defray the costs, but after some discussion with the dean, the idea was held in abeyance. The vicars had obtained an estimate of £40 to remove the partition, and intended to obtain a second for the removal of the gallery and the conservation of their library; when the gallery was installed does not seem to be recorded, but was presumably the one built during the days of Claver Morris's music club of the very early 18th century. Dean Armitage Robinson invited experts to come and look at the hall; their view was that there would originally have been a screens passage across the hall and it was necessary to retain it if aiming to return the hall to its medieval appearence. Despite this, the vicars decided to ignore the experts, remove the screen and to keep the later gallery at the west end with its staircase. All indications of earlier doors and windows were to be exposed and preserved. The Dean and Chapter made a grant of £25 and when the oriel window on to St Andrews Street showed signs of dislocation early in 1924 (it was thought due to heavy traffic), the vicars wrote to the Ecclesiastical Commissioners for help for both this and the general restoration; an offer of £125 was forthcoming. A year later, part of the original screen from the hall was discovered in No. 4 Vicars Close and removed and replaced in the hall. The restoration work started in 1925, with Mr Bray appointed as clerk of works, under the supervision of the cathedral architect, Sir Charles Nicolson, and a public appeal for funds was set up. A year later a similar appeal was launched in the USA. The final bill for the restoration work in the hall came to £819 13s.4d. and in 1929 notices were placed in the papers thanking all who had contributed.[8]

In 1926 the two medieval statues in the hall, together with the 'oak chest from the muniment room' were sent to the Victoria and Albert Museum for conservation and in return the museum asked to be allowed to exhibit the figures for five years. It then offered to make plaster casts of them to replace the originals while on loan and make some for sale to other institutions. The college agreed, provided neither the originals nor copies were photographed for commercial purposes. It received the casts in January 1927. They joined several documents relating to the history of the college, which had been framed and hung in the hall; this may have improved the visitor experience but was not good for the documents which became seriously faded over the years. The steward was asked to write to the Wells and Glastonbury museums to find out what vicars choral manuscripts they held and whether they would be willing to sell them back to the college. The college also investigated displaying the college silver in the hall, but it proved too costly to conserve and insure it. In 1929 the Ecclesiastical Commissioners ordered the raising of insurance cover for the hall to £3000, £450 for a single house in the Close and £650 for a double; within the hall, the insurance value for the furniture, fittings and pictures remained the same, but £300 was added to cover the stained glass.[9]

The whole contentious issue of a pension scheme for the vicars had been left in abeyance for the duration of the war, though preliminary discussions between the Chapter and the college had taken place. They were brought sharply into focus in November 1918. Fergus Asquith wished to resign from his position as a vicar choral after 40 years of service, but he also wished to receive a pension and retain his house. The college view was that either he remained a member of the college, with his house and all other emoluments, even if the Dean and Chapter dispensed with his services in the choir, or he resigned as a member and his future lay in the hands of Chapter. They were, however, willing to meet the Chapter to discuss the issue. Given that Asquith, despite his age (he had become a vicar in 1880) had been away on war work but refused to furnish particulars of the pay he had received from it, his resignation was declined on the grounds that the Chapter had no money to fund it, and he was asked to resume his duties in the following February, when he was released from National Service work. A year or so later, in November 1920, a much more satisfactory arrangement was made with the organist. Dr Davies' stipend was raised to £300 and a house, but provided he kept the latter, he was willing to give up £170 of his stipend to pay an assistant organist. This was something Chapter could agree to, but then, Davies was himself a member of Chapter. Thomas Davies had originally come to Wells in 1895 as a priest vicar, a post he resigned when he was made organist in 1899. In 1912 he was appointed a prebendary and became Precentor and Canon Residentiary in 1920, hence the need to re-organise his workload. This was unparalleled in any other cathedral of the old foundation; never before had an organist become a member of the Quinque Personae of the Chapter. Davies retired as organist in 1933, but retained his Chapter posts until his death in 1947.[10]

The whole vexed question of vicars' pensions rumbled on throughout the 1920s. Many of the prebendaries felt a duty of care towards the vicars and one of the ways that Chapter could have considered increasing their stipends was by use of the Supplementary Fund. This, however, was raised from lay subscribers and while anything to increase the efficiency of the choir was deemed suitable for a grant, Chapter felt this did not include supporting a system whereby members continued to hold positions which they could no longer fill satisfactorily. In 1922 when Albert Hodgkinson came to be perpetuated as a vicar, he was offered a bonus of £20 from the Fund if he agreed to certain conditions, namely: that he would resign his position voluntarily and without controversy if called on to do so by the Dean and Chapter on the grounds of inability to perform his duties and that he make a annual payment into a pension fund sufficient to provide a £10 annuity when he reached 60. A vicar who resigned on request because of inability would be guaranteed a pension of £60 inclusive of his £10. Hodgkinson declined the extra £20 on these conditions. He was nevertheless perpetuated. Chapter was offering what it felt possible, but the vicars were unwilling to concede the principle of a lifetime's job without stronger inducements. In the interim, the Priest Principal, the Revd. Hugh Parnell, had been working on a pension scheme which was approved by the college. The Hall minutes note that it was presented to the Dean and Chapter in 1925, where it met with theoretical approval, but Chapter felt it could not afford to implement it. However, no record of this appears in the Chapter minutes and nowhere are the terms of the scheme recorded. The same was true three years later when, in 1928 members of the college gave general approval to certain principles which were to form the basis of pension discussions with Chapter.[11]

Before any resolution of the pension problem was reached, something happened which changed things forever. In 1928 a church commission was set up to study the organisation and constitutions of cathedrals with a view to updating them and making them more uniform by a Cathedrals Measure. One of the proposed reforms was the dissolution of all the Church of England's minor corporate bodies in cathedral churches and the transfer of their possessions to the cathedral chapters or the Ecclesiastical Commissioners. When members of the commission visited Wells, the Dean and Chapter of

Wells objected vigorously to the proposed Measure which they regarded as a complete breach with the history of their church and a violation of the independence secured by their original constitution and guaranteed again by Queen Elizabeth's charter, which expressly empowered them to make such 'statutes and ordinances as needed', provided they conformed to the law of the land. One of the particular points they made was their objection to the dissolution of <u>all</u> minor corporations. While it might be desirable elsewhere, it would be disastrous at Wells. They maintained that the existence of the college enabled them to attract a better class of men than would otherwise be the case with the small stipend offered. Moreover, the vicars took a particular pride in their ancient Hall and Chapel, and with the help of benefactors had kept them in good condition at great cost. While Chapter felt their stipends should be increased as soon as possible, the dissolution of the college would be a 'cruel break with the past and great grief to themselves'. In addition it would involve much extra expense for which it appeared no provision had been made. With regard to the proposed transfer of property, they felt strongly that it should not be compulsory, but only undertaken at the request of the present holders. Needless to say, the vicars were equally adamant about retaining their ancient collegiate status. In a written report submitted to the commissioners they argued that they were not the equivalent of the lay clerks and singing men of the newer cathedrals. There were still a number of priest vicars and their lay colleagues had equal rights. It could not be said of them that they neglected their duties or that their fellowship was moribund. They declared they had transformed themselves, the Close and their hall in recent years and that while inside the Close they owed obedience to their own Seniors and Principals, outside it, they owed obedience to the Dean and Chapter, with the Bishop overseeing all. If abuses in other organisations justified their suppression, so be it, but why should Wells be included in a blanket suppression. They then set out their current financial position, arguing strongly that there was no controversy now between themselves and the Chapter, and there was machinery to deal with every contingency, but both sides lacked the money to implement them.[12] While there might have been disagreements between the college and Chapter, as in all families, an attack from outside united them.

Despite the strong objections from Wells and other ancient cathedrals, the Church Assembly passed the Cathedrals Measure in 1931. Each cathedral then negotiated separately over the exact changes to be made in its own case and the new constitution it would have. Among the general principles to be applied in the case of each cathedral was the provision of a pension scheme for any clergy other than the dean and canons, as well as laymen serving in the cathedral; the appointments of organist, choir and virgers etc were to continue to be made in the same manner as before; the compulsory transfer of all property belonging to minor corporations, with the goods and chattels going to the Dean and Chapter and any real property to the Ecclesiastical Commissioners, who would cease to pay any annual sum to such corporation, making it instead to the Chapter. It was open to any Dean and Chapter to reconstitute a minor corporation provided these principles remained intact. Each cathedral scheme was also to include terms of service, duties and remuneration of its vicars choral, and it would not affect the tenure of office or the rights of anyone currently holding office without his consent in writing to the Commission.

Not unnaturally, the college disagreed with almost all of this. The vicars were anxious to retain their collegiate status and wanted to petition Chapter to refuse all interference with it, as well as refusing to accept college property and annual receipts from the Ecclesiastical Commissioners. It was not, however, opposed to the vesting of its remaining property with the Commissioners. The main body of their formal response covered all aspects of their appointments, discipline, houses and stall duty by the priest vicars, but chiefly with the financial, freehold and pension aspects. The current lay vicars received a salary of £80 p.a. and a house; what they would like was an increase to £120 p.a. as well as the house. If, they argued, a pension scheme was in place, it would be reasonable to reduce the numbers of lay vicars to nine, three of each voice, and therefore costing Chapter only £100 p.a. more in salaries than at present. In return, they were willing to give up their freehold or life tenure of their post so that it could be converted into a pension scheme. They proposed that there should be two classes of vicar choral: those in possession of a stall and discharging their duties, and vicars *emeriti*, in possession of a stall but incapable of discharging the duties. In such case, a vicar would resign his stall, but be collated by the bishop to one of the Combe stalls with the dignity of vicar *emeritus*, and receive £60 p.a. by way of pension and remain in his house. If he left his house he would receive an extra £20 p.a.[13] These proposals may have reflected the general thinking of the college, but were unlikely to meet with the whole-hearted approval of Chapter. In the event, nothing happened at Wells for two years, leaving both Chapter and college with an uncomfortable period of uncertainty. In 1932, in the absence of definite information, the college agreed to carry on business as usual. Except, of course, this was not really possible. One of their first responses to the Measure had been to resolve to draw up a legal deed of gift giving one of their number, Harry Partridge, 'all our books, chattels in silver, brass and pewter in consideration and return for his services to this place', in effect, preventing their handover to the Chapter. At the end of 1932, the Theological College's lease of No. 27 in the Close expired and it requested a renewal. The college had to temporise because for some time to come, its legal status was uncertain and any new lease might prove invalid. In November the following year all the vicars' Close houses were inspected and their rents recorded with a view to their possible take-over by the Chapter, and the Chapter clerk was asked to draw up an inventory of all the vicars' property passing to the Chapter.

In 1933 the period of negotiation with the Cathedral Commissioners over the scheme for Wells eventually got under way. There were draft schemes, amendments, redrafts, interviews in London between the new dean, Henry Malden, who had just succeeded Armitage Robinson, and Sir Henry Sharp, one of the Commissioners, but the vicars played no real part in all of this. The vicar principal, the Rev. Hugh Parnell, who was also the college historian, resigned his post in March 1933, possibly because he felt that the Dean and Chapter were not fighting hard enough for the continuation of the college in some form. In March 1934 the vicars received a letter from the dean telling them that in the absence of any definitive scheme, in his personal opinion they should just carry on as usual. Even by October he was unable to give them any further information. In November 1934 a further printed draft scheme was submitted for the approval of the Dean and Chapter by the Commissioners. Asked for their views, the vicars suggested several alterations and after Chapter consideration the dean sent them on to Sir Henry Sharp. The final result was set out in two Orders in Council in 1935, one dealing with the vicars and one more generally with the new constitution for the cathedral. The College of Vicars Choral was to retain its name but have no corporate rights, possessions or duties in relation to that designation. The Chapel and Hall with all their contents, together with books, muniments, plate, pictures, pewter and any income arising from them were passed to the Dean and Chapter to be used as they thought fit for the use and benefit of the vicars choral. In other respects, the rights and privileges of the college would in future be such as the Chapter, subject to the statutes, might determine. The £880 p.a. previously paid by the Ecclesiastical Commissioners to the college in lieu of their landed endowments, would in future be paid to the Dean and Chapter. While some of the houses in the Close were and would continue to be, held by the Commissioners, those occupied by the vicars themselves, namely Nos. 2, 4-7, 9-11, 14-15, 17-18, 22-23, 27-28 would pass to the Dean and Chapter.[14]

Thus the College of Vicars Choral of Wells ceased to exist in anything but name. Yet the vicars still sing, live in the Close, celebrate the feast of their founder in their hall, using their ancient pewter, so in some ways little has changed. They no longer have responsibility for the upkeep of their Close, there are no priest vicars among them, but they now have improved stipends, pensions and the knowledge that, with the choristers, they form one of the finest cathedral choirs in the world.

APPENDIX I
THE VICARS' OATH

I, N..., late admitted into a perpetuall Vicary of ye Cathedral Churche of Welles, make my othe opon this holy boke that I fro hens forwardis schalbe obedient to ye principalys that now beth & to here successouris and to all berynge ye charge of poer [power] And to all my senyores in all that lawful is & honest after my poer schal fro hens kepe And schal as moche as in me is mak the same of other to be kept al the Statutes and laudable consuetudis of this place. And yt I schal nort discuver utwardis any of the statutes secretis and councellis of this place by ye wheche ther might disclaimdire or preiudice or greuance fal to any of my felischipe, and if any such greuance or disclaimder may come to my knewleche, I schal as feruorthe as I can or may let it. And if y may nort I schall lete the pricipalys haue ther of knewleche and wetynge. Also by my poer I schall helpe and mayntayne and to do other to mayntayne al maner of lyvelodys [livelihoods] rentys and seruicis perteynynge to this place and of right longynge to this place, and therto be helper to defend and recuver hit fro al enemyes and never consent to delyuer hit to other use And if it fortune me her after to be promotyd fro this worshupfull place wher euyr y comm or abyd I schall auyr be in worde and dede & wyll a welwylled trew frende And in al thynges to this place perteynynge be behofull and diligent helper as god me bidys, and by this boke. Amen.[1]

APPENDIX II
THE VICARS' PAINTING

There is no reference to the painting in the records of the college. There is nothing about its commission in the Act Book which ends in 1593; the next volume of acts does not begin until 1624. The account for 1591/2 – the only one for the 1590s – is badly damaged and that part which can be read appears to contain nothing relevant and is anyway almost certainly too early to record payment for the completed painting.[1] Godwin's book, published in 1601, contains the first mention of it under his entry for Ralph of Shrewsbury.[2]

'This man is famous for the first foundation of our Vicars close in Wels. The memory of which benefit is to be seene expressed in a picture up[on] the wal at the foot of the hall staires. In it the Vicars kneeling, seeme to request the Bishop in these words:

'Per vicos positi villae, pater alme rogamus
Ut simul uniti, te dante domos maneamus'
Disperst about the towne, we humbly pray
Together, through thy bounty dwell we may
He answereth them thus:
'Vestra petunt merita, quod sint concessa petita
Ut maneatis ita, loca fecimus hic stabilata'
For your demaund, deserts do plead, I will do what you crave,
To this purpose established, here dwellings you shall have.

This picture being now almost worne out, at what times of late yeares, the Vicars by the gratious favour of Her Majesty had their revenues confirmed to them, being in danger to be spoyled of them by certaine sacrilegious cormorants, they likewise caused a picture of excellent workmanship to be drawen, containing a memorial of both the one and the other'.

Godwin thus makes it quite clear that there were two paintings. It is, however, slightly ambiguous as to whether the second was a new one or a complete or partial overpainting of the first. It is possible that the first painting was a wall painting at the foot of the stairs. Godwin also suggested that the original may have been painted soon after 1348, which is possible if it was indeed a wall painting. If he meant that the painting as we now know it was a re-painting then this dating is unlikely, though it may perhaps date back to the refounding of the college by Bishop Bekynton in the mid-fifteenth century. The top left hand section of the painting, showing Bishop Ralph and the original vicars, has a 15th century look to it. If this is indeed the case, then the group portrait is of even more historical interest. It is also worth noting that Godwin, who became a canon in 1585, refers to 'sacriligeous cormorants'.

Beside the portraits of the Elizabethan vicars, is an inscription, again in Latin, which Godwin does not quote because it had no relevance to Bishop Ralph. In translation it reads:

'What Ralph bequeathed in pious zeal
When we lived far and wide
Good Bishop Bekynton increases
With grace and wealth beside.
Now in these days Elizabeth
Hath stablished us in all
Good Queen, may thy life be very long
Thy sceptre never fall!'[3]

The painting, which measures 1880 mm x 1820 mm, was conserved in 2007 by Helen White of the National Portrait Gallery.[4] Dendrochronology was attempted at the time but the wood of the panels is cut in such a way that there are not enough rings to make dating possible. The expert opinion was that the layers of paint were so fragile that an attempt to determine the existence of any under-painting would not be productive. It is also clear from the nature of the panels that this was the original size of the picture. If, and it is a very big if, the top left hand corner was a 15th cent. painting, then just possibly the remainder of the panel held an image of saints which the Protestant vicars of Elizabeth's reign thought should be painted over.

The painting originally hung on the processional staircase from the Close up to the hall (as Godwin says) and in the 19th century was moved inside to hang above the hall fireplace. Neither location was chosen with its physical well-being in mind. It was re-framed in 1862, probably at the time it was moved inside. Following its conservation it now hangs on the east wall of the hall.[5]

APPENDIX III
THE PAYMENT OF VICARS

The way that an individual vicar was paid was not straightforward, and altered over the centuries. The information provided here has appeared at the appropriate places in the text, but is brought together for convenience in an attempt to make a coherent account of the different sources of income. In the earliest days, each vicar choral's stipend was the responsibility of the individual canon whose deputy he was. At this period, the income from his prebend provided a canon on average with 10 marks p.a.; from that he had to pay his vicar 2-3 marks p.a. If a vicar progressed from minor orders to full priesthood, it often made a difference to his stipend.[1] When Bishop Jocelin, as part of his enhancement of offices at Wells, assigned the church of Wedmore to the deanery in about 1210, the priest vicar at Wells was to receive 4 marks p.a. from the said prebend, while the church of Wookey, previously the dean's, became the prebend for the sub-dean, who was charged with paying his vicar 2 marks p.a.[2] Although his stipend [later often referred to as stall wages] formed the major part of a medieval vicar's income, he did receive one or two supplements to it. In the early 13th century, both canons and vicars received a bread allowance every other day, but as part of his reforms of the administration at Wells, in 1242 Bishop Jocelin issued an ordinance whereby a vicar would receive 1d. per day in lieu of bread, provided he was present at matins and the other canonical hours or had permission to be absent (a canon received 2d.). The rest of his food was either provided by the household of his canon, or had to be paid for out of his stipend.

Vicars were also entitled to a share of commons, (food and money from the cathedral's surplus funds after all necessaries had been paid for) when the claims of the dignitaries and resident canons had been satisfied. The earliest surviving Chapter accounts, probably for the year 1292 show £66 18s.10d. being paid to the vicars to be divided amongst them.[3] In addition, increasing numbers of clergy and pious laymen left money or charges on their estate for anniversary services, known as obits, to be said in the cathedral for the good of their souls. To take just one example, in 1235, Roger, one of the canons, granted his houses in Wells to the Chapter, with a charge of 10s. p.a. to be paid to the canons and vicars present at his obit.[4] If the obit took the form of a daily, weekly or annual mass, then the priest saying the mass, often a priest vicar, was paid to do so. In addition, a payment was distributed among all the clergy and vicars who attended such a mass and since the number of obits was many, even attendance at a select few meant the cash payments made a significant contribution to each vicar's income. There is little doubt that at this period, vicars could live comfortably on their income.

When an act of parliament abolished chantries in 1547, both the jobs of the chantry priests and the obit payments vanished. All this chantry income was now diligently collected by the king's receiver each year: for the year 1550/1 Master John Aylworthe received well over a hundred pounds from the Chapter in total; the proportion due to the Crown from obits was assessed at £48 1s. 4d., much of which would previously have gone to priest vicars or other chantry chaplains. From henceforth, after he had paid the crown dues, the escheator divided the balance of the income over and above what was required to fund the masses and obits, a sum of about £20, equally among canons, vicars and choristers, but this was only a small amount of what they had previously received. However, while much of the money earmarked for the obits and anniversaries was paid to the Crown, the lands and property which provided a large proportion of this income remained in the hands of the Chapter who leased them and thus benefited from all increases in rents and fines on grants of new leases and divided any surplus among themselves; the vicars and choristers should have received a proportion of this as well, but how much and how often depended on the decisions of the Chapter. The escheator also received what came in from weddings and burials to add to the total. This system was known as 'escheatery'. The income from it, never great, also fluctuated year by year depending on how many leases were renewed. The Chapter was not unmindful of the financial hardship felt by the vicars and sometimes granted them extra sums 'on account of the poverty and scantiness of their stipends'.[5]

The reduction of their income after 1547 was balanced for the vicars by the amount of time now at their own disposal because of the huge reduction of daily services under Protestantism. It is from the mid 16th century, therefore, that the pattern of the vicars' lives took on the shape familiar to vicars today as their increased free time enabled them to seek part-time employment. Sometimes this was working for the Chapter itself in posts such as master of the fabric, communar, or escheator, which meant that much of the financial management of the cathedral was in the hands of vicars, keeping the college closely tied to the affairs of the Chapter. For many vicars employment took the form of teaching, but any other work for which an individual was competent was accepted. As long as they were present for the services, the Chapter had no interest in how they spent the rest of their time provided that they did nothing that brought the cathedral into disrepute.

During the sixteenth century the number of vicars were considerably reduced. From a high point in late Middle Ages of 40-50, in the years following the Reformation the number of vicars usually fluctuating from between 20 and 24 and then for most of Elizabeth's reign stabilised at between 15 and 17. At Wells, as everywhere, vicars choral suffered from financial distress. Their resources failed to keep pace with inflation and many now had to provide for wives and families as well. The Chapter did not ignore their difficulties and gave them each an extra £3 6s.8d. a year in lieu of the meat and drink to which they were entitled to receive from their canons and doubled their holiday allowance from three weeks to six in 1584. The vicars' main source of income, however, was their stipend. By this point, the stipends were no longer paid by individual canons to 'their' vicar. There were thirty canonical stalls, each paying the equivalent of the vicarial wages into the Chapter's common fund. The vicars were then paid from an allocation of £76 from this fund, priest vicars receiving £3 p.a. and the other vicars £2. At the beginning of Elizabeth's reign, her Visitors ordered that the establishment should not exceed 20 vicars and that all should receive £3 p.a. If the numbers fell below 20, then the unexpended balance was to be divided equally between the vicars in post. The remainder of the sum of £76 reverted to the common fund and Chapter used part of it to pay the salary of the schoolmaster and a regular 26s.8d. p.a. went to the choristers. If Chapter so chose, it could also distribute some or all of what was left among the vicars according to who had been present at the major religious feasts.[6] On the death or resignation of a vicar, his stipend was reallocated to the most senior vicar until the vacancy was filled.

The final source of income for the vicars was their own estate. On his appointment, each vicar was collated by the bishop to a house in the Close, the free accommodation forming a not insubstantial part of his remuneration. The reduction of numbers of vicars following the Reformation left large numbers of the houses untenanted and the situation was stabilised by allowing each vicar not one, but two houses, the second one nominally for his 'chattels'. Some vicars leased the second house, the rent helping to augment their income, or in a few cases amalgamated the two properties to form one house large enough to accommodate a family. Since this was an expensive undertaking, many leased out both houses and rented somewhere for them and their families in town. The endowment of his new college in terms of estates in various parishes and properties in Wells itself in 1348 by Bishop Ralph of Shrewsbury, augmented by later benefactors, had been intended to support the communal life of the college. The maintenance of the hall and offices, the vicars' houses, the payment of college servants and the provision of food for communal dining all came out of these common funds. The estates were naturally subject to the standard taxes levied on landowners such as tenths, land tax and poor rates.[7] What the income from the estates was not intended to do was augment the vicars' personal stipends. Needless to say, that was what much of it was used for. By the mid 18th century, for instance, each vicar received two shillings per week for commons [£5 6s. p.a.], since they no longer ate communally, and a further £1 p.a. to top up his stipend.[8]

The Cathedrals Commission Report of 1854 gives a clear picture of the financial arrangements of the vicars. The priest vicars received a small quarterly stipend of £1 14s.11d. which was paid out of capitular funds, that is, just under £7 p.a., slightly less than the two senior choristers ' payment of £10 p.a. This was augmented by payments for preaching and for dealing with baptisms, marriages and burial services, but not the regular services. The lay vicars got a similar stipend, and some were able to augment it with non-liturgical posts within the cathedral or any external job consistent with their singing duties. The Report makes clear that stipends had barely increased since the 16th century. It also noted under the lay vicars' heading that the remainder of their income came from the rents and fines on the renewal of leases of their corporate estates.

The rents formed the most regular part of the income, though there were often arrears and occasional defaults. When a lease was granted it was usually for three lives, that is three people named as successive lessees and the lease ran until the death of the last surviving lessee. On the death of each lessee a heriot was due to the college, and while it had customarily been made in the form of crops or the 'best beast' in a herd or flock, by the nineteenth century it was almost always a money payment. When a lease was granted, or new lives were added to an existing lease, a fine, or substantial cash payment based on the value of the property was due to the college. It was therefore very difficult to judge the average annual income because of the considerable variables; some years a number of fines were paid for leases or additional lives, in other years perhaps none. Over a long period, it was suggested that perhaps the average income was £80, but at times it was so small as to leave the vicars in 'painful and straightened circumstances'. In contrast, the canons had a generous regular income. Both groups had free accommodation and the canons had nine months of the year free to augment their income. The vicars had, perforce, to earn their extra money in Wells or close by. It is hardly surprising, therefore, that the vicars had explored the possibility of handing over their estates to the Ecclesiastical Commissioners in return for a fixed annual sum. In 1852 the Commissioners declined, but when the subject was re-opened in 1866, at a time when they were taking over the capitular estates, this time an agreement was reached. The vicars handed over all their land and property in return for a regular annual payment of £880.[9]

APPENDIX IV
THE CLAVER MORRIS LAWSUIT, 1725

The dispute between Dr Claver Morris and the College of Vicars Choral has considerable significance in the physical history of Vicars' Close. The background is set out in some detail in a petition that the vicars made to the court of Chancery and the following account is taken from that, interspersed with comments from Dr Morris's diary.[1]

At the time of the petition in 1725 the Close was bounded on the north by College Lane, on the east by a canonical house (now Tower House) in the possession of Dr Creyghton, the precentor, on the west by another canonical house formerly in the possession of the archdeacon of Wells but occupied by Mr Piers, and on the south by the street now known as St Andrew's Street. The only entrance to the Close was through the south gate. There was also an outer wall along the east and west perimeters on to which the back courts of the vicars' houses abutted. The difficulties go back to the period of the Commonwealth when the Parliamentary Visitors granted the vacant houses to tradesmen and people of all sorts, who had no interest to keeping it as a Close. They opened posterns, back doors and shop windows as suited their convenience. Following the Restoration in 1660, the vicars sought and obtained the bishop's licence to let some of the houses in the worst condition on repairing leases, but the licence also states that all posterns, backdoors (i.e. through the perimeter walls) etc were to be walled up and that in future no posterns etc should be made in any leased house.

Two houses in the north east corner (nos. 21 & 22 on the east side, now no. 13) remained unleased and ruinous until 1670, when Francis Poulet offered to take them on if he could have an entrance through the north wall of the Close. The bishop gave his licence and Poulet was granted a 21year lease. Exactly how ruinous the houses in fact were is an interesting point. Today, no. 13 does not give the appearance of a new-built house of the late 17th century. Like no. 14 opposite, it is L-shaped, with a wing adjacent to the chapel, and the wings of both houses have much in common architecturally, both appearing late medieval or early Tudor. It may perhaps be that the interior was ruinous but the external walls survived sufficiently to form the basis of a restoration. Poulet rebuilt the houses and his lease allowed him to cut a passage into their back courts and also, and more importantly, a door from College Lane through the wall into his front garden from whence there was access to the Close; the licence specified that it was to be only for the use of Poulet and his family and otherwise was to be kept locked. The lease had already been renewed when Poulet's widow died in 1694. Her administrators were her brother and Precentor Creyghton, and the latter renewed the lease again but the covenant relating to ingress and egress was omitted because Creyghton intended to wall up the doors, which he duly did. He then assigned the lease to his son-in-law, Dr Layng, who in turn renewed the lease with the covenant omitted because it was apparently no longer relevant. The long-term under-tenant of the house during this period was a man named Slade. He in turn sub-let to Claver Morris. Since Morris did not live there himself, he must also have had tenants. All these levels of rack-renting were not uncommon, but the loser was the college, which received only the first rent from Layng, while he, Slade and Morris were all making additional profits.

In 1708 Morris prevailed on Slade, with or without the knowledge of Creyghton and Layng, to allow him to open up the two closed doors. Slade had no right to give such permission, but Morris took the precaution in June 1709 of obtaining Dr Creyghton's leave to do so and a few days later he notes 'Obtained My Lord Bishop Hooper's Connivance at my making a Way into Close Hall'. Ignorant of these nods and winks by their superiors, when the vicars learned of it, they complained to the bishop. Bishop Hooper had a quiet word with Morris as a friend, telling him that if any formal complaint was made, he would not in justice be able to support him. Morris persisted. Early in 1710 Morris called upon the bishop in an attempt to get him to change his mind. His argument was that former bishops had granted Poulet the right to a door into College Lane and there were no college statutes forbidding the integrity of the Close to be breached. Bishop Hooper would not back down and the interview ended with a row. The biggest unanswered question of the whole affair is why Morris was so insistent on having the way opened up. He did not live there himself, nor did it provide a much quicker route from his own home to the cathedral and town. In 1711 Layng again renewed his lease with the vicars, and it had the same omission as to the privilege granted to Poulet, but included a clause prohibiting any common way or passage out of College Lane into the Close. The vicars would have been wiser to have insisted that all doors to College Lane were to be blocked up as well as prohibiting any common way, but possibly Layng would then not have renewed. It may be that some of the vicars sided with the lessees and could see no reason why there should not be a door to the lane. Layng then proceeded to assign the lease to Morris. When Morris himself came to renew the lease in 1718, both earlier clauses were omitted, so, as the vicars themselves admitted, tending to establish a freedom of passage to Morris and his subtenants from College Lane to the town. However, they claimed that some of their own number 'promoted Morris's design in breach of the privileges and liberties of their Society'.

Nothing much happened during the lifetime of the lease [Morris's leases seemed so far to have been for 7 rather than 21 years]. In September 1725, when he came to renew it, he persuaded the vicars to make it for 21 years; it also omitted any clause referring to doors into the lane. He refers to seven of the vicars visiting him, together with their steward in 1725, bringing with them the renewed lease to be executed. He duly executed its counterpart and paid the fine and fees. Morris then made it clear that he regarded that he had established the way from College Lane through Close Hall Walk as a common thoroughfare that anybody could use. A few months later in 1725, the vicars visited him again, asking that the lease be cancelled and another one drawn up with a covenant against having a door into Mr Pierce's 'backside', that is, back yard. Morris refused to agree to this, whereupon the vicars then announced that they should all have keys to Morris's passage, another request that was refused. Their lease book, however, records a licence from the bishop in 1725 for Morris to give a key to Mrs Elizabeth Irish to go from College Lane through his two gardens in to the Close. The vicars had recourse to the bishop. In November 1725 another deputation visited the doctor, demanding that the door or passageway be stopped up or they would take him to court with the bishop's financial support. They admitted that there had never been a clause in any previous lease, to Morris or any other tenant to this effect. When Morris refused to back down, the vicars set up a bar and post to block the passage. He cut it down, and threatened to sue the vicars for setting it up in the first place. This, the vicars feared, would ruin them. They begged the court of Chancery to stay Morris's proceeding against them while they gathered their witnesses, many of them aged and infirm, and set out their testimony to prove their case.

Morris's legal position was that the lease granted him the house and appurtenances and that since he had made the way through himself this must be deemed an appurtenance to his house and passed to him by the grant in his lease. He further argued that the original institution of the Close and its rules and orders and restrictive covenants did not apply to him. All that was relevant was his present lease and to justify his position he had cut down the bar. Like many legal cases, the formal result is not known, but the fact that the passage remains open suggests success for the doctor. The whole issue is a good example of the lack of financial acumen and good legal advice which dogged the business affairs of the college.

NOTES

Chapter 1 : Beginnings

[1] Frank Harrison, *Music in Medieval Britain* (1958), pp. 46-7; *Calendar of the Documents of the Dean and Chapter of Wells Cathedral*, Historical Manuscripts Commission, vol. 1 (1907), pp. 255, 530, 531, hereafter cited as *Cal.* vol.1; the entries here calendared are from the earliest Wells cartulary, known as *Liber Albus I* (ref. DC/CF 2/1).

[2] Kathleen Edwards, *The English Secular Cathedrals in the Middle Ages* (2nd ed., 1967), pp.135-6.

[3] Strictly speaking the term 'vicars choral' was not used until the late 15th century; earlier than that the singing men were usually referred to as 'vicars perpetual' or just 'vicars'.

[4] In the context of Wells, the word 'quire' denotes that part of the church where the daily liturgy took place; the word 'choir' denotes those who sang it.

[5] Harrison, *op.cit.* p. 51, 104-5. For full details of the Wells Consuetudinary, see A. Watkin (ed), *Dean Cosyn and Wells Cathedral Miscellanea*, Somerset Record Society, vol. 56 (1941), pp. 27-52.

[6] Roger Bowers, L.S. Colchester and Anthony Crossland, *Organs and Organists of Wells Cathedral* (1998), pp. 1-2.

[7] *Calendar of the Documents of the Dean and Chapter of Wells Cathedral*, Historical Manuscripts Commission, 2 vols. (1907, 1914), hereafter cited as *Cal.* vol.1, *Cal.* vol.2); *Cal.* vol. 2, p. 618.

[8] *Cal.* vol. 1, p. 122.

[9] Edwards, *op.cit.*, pp.265-270; *Cal.* vol. 1, p.530; Watkin , *Dean Cosyn*, pp. 5-6

[10] L.S. Colchester, *Wells Cathedral School* (1985); Nicholas Orme, *The Minor Clergy of Exeter Cathedral, 1300-1545* (Exeter, 1980), p.xvii.; A.J. Scrase, 'Who were the vicars choral at Wells c. 1200-1380', *Somerset Archaeological and Natural History Society*, vol. 158 (2015).

[11] *Cal.* vol. 1, pp. 164-5, 204, 252-4, 377. It is from entries such as these in the cartulary that we can attempt to identify the whereabouts of the many altars and chapels in the medieval cathedral. For further details of the various chantries and the vicars who served them, see Watkin, *Dean Cosyn*, pp. 18-20.

[12] *Cal.* vol. 1, pp. 74, 162.

[13] *Ibid.*, pp. 148, 225, 239, 240, 535.

[14] *Ibid.*, pp. 74-5, 82, 131.

[15] *Ibid.*, pp. 133, 142.

[16] *Ibid.*, pp. 191, 208.

[17] *Ibid.*, pp.159,193, 222; see also Scrase, *op.cit.*

[18] Watkin, *Dean Cosyn*, pp. 11-16.

[19] *Ibid.*, p. 20.

[20] *Ibid.*, pp. 21-4.

[21] Frederick Harrison, *Life in a Medieval College: The Story of the Vicars Choral of York Minster* (1952), p. 23; Barrie Dobson, Introduction, *Vicars Choral at English Cathedrals*, ed. Richard Hall and David Stocker (Oxford, 2005), p. 3.

[22] *Ibid.*, Chapter 11; Warwick Rodwell, with Frances Neale, ' "Begun While the Black Death Raged..." The Vicars' Close at Wells', pp.112-3.

[23] *Cal.* vol. 1, p. 219.

Chapter 2 : The Foundation of the College

[1] VC/CF/2/1-2. These two documents are the earliest records of the college. They and others have been transcribed and translated by L.S. Colchester in 'Documents 1348-1600 of the Vicars Choral of Wells', unpublished booklet, pp. 1-2; Edwards, *English Secular Cathedrals*, p. 284.

[2] All passages relating to the buildings of Vicars' Close draw extensively on the archaeological work of Professor Warwick Rodwell, and a more comprehensive architectural study can be found in his work, with Frances Neale,' "Begun While the Black Death Raged..." The Vicars' Close at Wells' in *Vicars Choral at English Cathedrals, op.cit.*

[3] *Age of Chivalry: Art in Plantagenet England, 1200-1400*, ed. J. Alexander and P. Binski (Royal Academy of Arts, 1987), nos. 526-7.

[4] *Cal.* vol. 1, p. 215

[5] VC/CF/2/2; Colchester *op.cit.*; Elsa van der Zee, *Wells Cathedral: an architectural and historical guide* (2012), p. 176

[6] Printed translation in J.H. Parker, *Architectural Antiquities of the City of Wells* (1866), p. 31.

[7] *Cal.* vol. 2, p. 618.

[8] A. Watkin (ed), *Dean Cosyn* op. cit., pp. 139-49. The statutes are in Latin and are not translated, but see H.E.Reynolds, *Wells Cathedral: its foundation, constitutional history and statutes* (1881), based on Nathaniel Chyles' s 'History', MS, c. 1680, which used Lambeth MS 729, Liber Ruber (DC/CF 2/2) and other mss.

[9] VC/CF 1/1 ; transcribed and translated by L.S. Colchester, 'Register of the Vicars Choral of Wells, 1393 – 1534', unpublished booklet. In fact Bekynton got his date wrong – the earliest entry is dated 12 Jan. 1393/4.

[10] For the full text of the oath, see Appendix 1.

[11] Colchester, 'Register'.

[12] *ibid.*, pp.5-7, 9; *Cal.* vol.1, pp.262, 273.

[13] 'Register', pp. 4-6; *Cal.* vol.1, p. 304.

[14] 'Register', p. 11; VC/Hist/2 (transcription of accounts, 1420-25 by Sir H.C. Maxwell-Lyte); VC/CF 2/29; VC/MISC/5

[15] 'Register', pp.10-11.

[16] *ibid.*, pp. 11-12, 18-19.

[17] *ibid.*, p.12.

[18] *ibid.*, pp. 3, 13, 19; Rodwell, *Vicars Choral at English Cathedrals*, pp.117-8, 123; VC/Hist/2; H. Parnell, *The College of Vicars Choral Wells* (1926), p.19.

[19] *Cal.* vol. 2, pp. 626, 631, 639-41; VC/Hist/2; Julian D. Richards, *The Vicars Choral of York Minster: The College at Bedern* (2001), p. 383.

[20] *The Register of Thomas Bekynton, Bishop of Bath and Wells, 1443-1465*, ed. Sir H.C. Maxwell-Lyte and M.C.B. Dawes, pt 1 (Somerset Record Society, vol. 49, 1934), pp. 51-2; see note 8 above; *Cal.* vol. 2, p. 71.

[21] Watkin, *Dean Cosyn*, pp. 99, 103 ff; Harrison, *Music in Medieval Britain*, p. 10; *Cal.* vol. 1, p.406; *Bekynton Register*, p. xiv.

[22] Colchester, 'Register', p. 24; *Bekynton Register*, pp. 338-9.

[23] Rodwell, *Vicars Choral at English Cathedrals*, pp. 128,135; Elsa van der Zee, *Wells Cathedral*, p.176.

[24] *Cal.* vol. 1, pp. 490, 498-502; Lady Hungerford, who had inherited the manor from her father, Lord Botreaux, was raising money to pay off debts incurred for the ransom of her son Robert, Lord Hungerford, captured at the battle of Castillon, the final defeat of the English in the Hundred Years War, in 1453; *Bekynton Register*, pp. xv, xvi.

[25] Colchester, 'Documents', pp. 5-6.

Chapter 3 : To the Reformation and Beyond

[1] I am grateful to Mrs Frances Neale for making this point as part of her work of transcribing the cartulary (VC/CF1/2).

[2] Bowers, Colchester and Crossland, *Organs and Organists of Wells Cathedral*, op. cit. pp.1-3; Harrison, *Music in Medieval Britain*, op. cit., pp. 202-8.

[3] L.S. Colchester, 'Communars' Accounts, 1327-1600', unpublished booklet (1984), p. 58.

[4] Colchester, 'Register', pp.19, 28-9; *Cal.* vol. 2, pp. 9, 97, 101, 106, 113, 115, 110, 128-9, 173, 211, 685 *et aliis*; 'Communars' Accounts', pp. 95 103, 109, 117, 124, 132, 140.

[5] *Bekynton Register*, p. 328; 'Communars' Accounts', p. 140; Stanford E. Lehmberg, *The Reformation of Cathedrals: Cathedrals in English Society, 1485-1603* (1988), pp. 9-12.

[6] DC/MUS 2/2; *Organs and Organists*, p. 25; 'Communars' Accounts', p. 171; *Cal.* vol. 2 p. 104.

[7] *ibid.*, pp. 200, 205, 207, 208, 220, 231, 248, 270; 'Communars' Accounts', p. 193;   *Organs and Organists*, pp. 26-7; Lehmberg, *Reformation of Cathedrals*, p. 210.

[8] *Cal.* vol 2, pp.121, 206, 301; Colchester, 'Register', pp. 29-30.

[9] Rodwell, *Vicars Choral at English Cathedrals*, pp. 126-7; Elsa van der Zee, *Wells Cathedral*, pp. 167- 171.

[10] Lehmberg, *Reformation of Cathedrals*, pp. 68-9.

[11] *Cal.* vol. 1, p. 376, *Cal.* 2, p.263; 'Communars' Accounts', p. 223; see also R.V. Sellars, 'The Chantry College in the Mountroy at Wells', *Wells Natural History and Archaeology Society Report*, 1959-60.

[12] It is not proposed to study the history of the College estates in any detail. This has already been done: see Robert G. Hill, 'The Estates of the Vicars Choral of Wells Cathedral, 1591-1866', MA Dissertation, University of Bristol (1998); *Valor Ecclesiasticus*, (1535, repr. 1810) vol. 1, pp. 137-9.

[13] L.S. Colchester, 'Act Book 1541-1593 of the Vicars Choral of Wells', unpublished booklet (1986), pp. 5, 10-12; the pages of the book before conservation were seriously damaged by damp and the entries frequently only partially legible; VC/HIST/2 ; A. Scrase, 'The Urban Estate of the Vicars Choral at Wells', ms in the cathedral archives information files.

[14] *Cal.* vol. 2, pp. 274, 276, 287; 'Communar's Accounts', pp. 228, 248, 253; Peter le Huray, *Music and the Reformation in England, 1549-1660* (Cambridge, 1968), p. 102.

[15] *Cal.* vol. 2, pp. 280-1; Lehmberg, *Reformation of Cathedrals*, pp.101-2, 124, 134; Colchester, 'Act Book', p. 14.

[16] Lehmberg, *Reformation of Cathedrals*, pp. 140, 142.

[17] *ibid.*, p. 301; Chapter Act Book, DC/CF 6/3f. 20; Colchester, 'Act Book', pp.21-23, 33, 39-40; *Cal.* vol. 2, p. 301.

[18] *ibid.*, pp. 313-4; Colchester, 'Act Book', pp.56-8.

[19] *ibid.*, p. 143; *Cal.* vol. 2, p.348; DC/E9/3 f. 193; Watkins Shaw, *The Succession of Organists from c. 1538* (1991), pp. 284-5.

[20] *Cal.* vol.2, p. 302; 'Act Book', pp. 39-41; Peter le Huray, *Music and the Reformation in England, 1549-1660* (1968), p. 267; Lehmberg, *Reformation of Cathedrals*, pp.190-1. Further details of Wells organists can be found in Philip

Barnes, 'The Music and Musicians of Wells Cathedral to 1859', (University of Manchester M.Mus. thesis, 1984).

[21] *Cal.* vol.2, pp. 2, 117,119; DC/CF 2/2, Liber Ruber, ff. 183, 197; Lehmberg, *Reformation of Cathedrals*, pp.218-9; le Huray, *Music and the Reformation*, pp. 40-42; DC/ADM 1/26, 51.

[22] Watkin, *Dean Cosyn*, op. cit., p. xxix; Colchester, *Act Book*, p.50.

[23] Episcopal register of Bishop Berkeley, Somerset Heritage Centre D/D/breg/15 f.18 ; Colchester, *Act Book*, pp. 24-30.

[24] *ibid.*, pp. 41; *Cal.* vol.2, pp. 294-5, 340.

[25] Colchester, *Act Book*, pp. 50-1.

[26] DC/ADM 1/28.

[27] DC/CF3/392; VC/CF2/242.

Chapter 4 : Revolution and Restoration

[1] The translation used here is VC/HIST/1 and dates from 1889.

[2] For further details of the painting, see Appendix 2.

[3] DC/CF12/223, 228; *Cal.* vol.2, p. 357; D.S. Bailey (ed) *Wells Cathedral Chapter Act Book 1663-1683*, Somerset Record Society, vol. 72 (1973), p. xxxii.

[4] VC/CF4/1; *Crown Revenues from Somerset and Dorset, 1605*, ed. Colin Brett, Somerset Record Society, vol.96 (2012), p. 153.

[5] Chapter Act Book, DC/CF 6/5 f.57; *Cal.* vol.2, pp. 354, 364, 376-7, 384-5, 389, 390, 413.

[6] *Cal.* vol. 2, pp. 376-7; Ledger Book G, p. 256; see Watkins Shaw, *The Succession of Organists*, pp.286-7, for a biography of Oker and 'John Oker: An Organist or a Dynasty', A.J. Scrase, *Somerset and Dorset Notes & Queries*, xxxv (2003), p. 255.

[7] DC/CF 6/6, f.122d; DC/CF 6/7, f. 176.

[8] *Ibid.*, p. 411; DC/CF 6/6 f. 168d.

[9] *Cal.* vol. 2, pp. 394, 400, 429; DC/CF 6/6, ff. 47, 53, 117-8, 176v; Stanford E. Lehmberg, *Cathedrals Under Siege: Cathedrals in English Society, 1600-1700* (Exeter, 1996), pp. 176-7.

[10] DC/CF6/7, f.96.

[11] Anthony Nott, *Under God's Visitation: A Study of the City of Wells from the Civil War to the Restoration* (Wells, 2010), p. 149. Nott's account also includes details of the various fates of the residentiary canons. The ten vicars who signed were Francis Standish, Arthur Alderley, William Atkins, Thomas Beaumont, Augustine Benford, Daniel Davis, James Dewbery, Anthony Mowrie, Henry Pope and Martin Symonds; A.G. Matthews (ed), *'A Revision of*

John Walker's Sufferings of the Clergy during the Grand Rebellion 1642-1660' (1948), p. 16.

[12] *Ibid.,* p. 147

[13] S.C. Newton, *Short Guides to Records: Parliamentary Surveys.*

[14] VC/E 1/1; Hill, 'Estates of the Vicars Choral', pp. 22, 63. At the time of the survey, eight of the vicars in the previous note were still in the Close. Dewbery and Mowrie were dead, but their widows were still resident. The four vicars who did not sign the 1646 petition, John Bicknall, John Moss, John Oker and Anthony Walkley were also still living there.

[15] Nott, *Under God's Visitation,* p. 158, n.32. By 1658 only Benford, Symonds, Atkins, Beaumont, Standish, Davis and Alderley were in receipt of stipends, see Matthews, *'Walker Revision',* p. 16.

[16] DC/F2/16, DC/F5/13, DC/ADM 1/212; *Wells Cathedral: A History,* ed. L.S. Colchester (repr. 1996), pp. 161-2.

[17] *Cal.* vol. 2, pp. 433-4, 337; the series of college act books does not resume until 1748 (VC/CF 4/2), leaving a gap of more than a century, between 1628 and 1748, so clearly more than one volume has gone missing. This leaves only the accounts and estate records as source material for the period from the vicars' own archive and even they have survived only patchily.

[18] Hill, 'Estates of the Vicars Choral', pp. 22-23.

[19] VC/CF 2/116.

[20] VC/F1/21 passim; Rodwell, *Vicars Choral at English Cathedrals,* p. 120.

[21] The pewter is still used each year at the commemoration breakfast held in November to celebrate the foundation of the college.

[22] E.A. Jones, 'The Silver and Pewter of the Vicars Choral at Wells', *Burlington Magazine* (Apr. 1936), pp. 280-5; Bailey, *Chapter Act Book,* pp. xxxii-xxxiii.

[23] *Cal.* vol.2, pp. 452-3; Watkins Shaw, *The Succession of Organists,* p. 287-8; the collection of part books [DC/MUS 1/11-13] were studied in detail by Philip Barnes, 'The Music and Musicians of Wells Cathedral to 1859', M Mus thesis, Manchester 1984, a copy of which is held in the Library.

[24] *Ibid.,* p. 288; *Cal.*vol. 2, pp. 463-4.

[25] *Cal.* vol. 2., pp. 456-8.

Chapter 5: Stagnation and Complacency?

[1] *Cal.* vol.2, pp. 500-3, 508-10, 531.

[2] *Ibid.,* pp. 346-7, 479-80, 522, 531; *The Diary of a West Country Physician, 1684-1726,* ed. Edmund Hobhouse (1934), p.15, 68.

[3] *Cal.* vol. 2, pp. 488, 478, 495, 503, 517.

[4] DC/MUS 1/11/1-59.

[5] See Barnes, 'Music and Musicians of Wells', pp.17-19; K. Long, *The Music of the English Church* (1972) (quoted Barnes).

[6] *Diary of a West Country Physician* pp. 41, 52, 94, 107, 110, 113, 125.

[7] VC/E3/6 pp. 139, 142; for details of the dispute, see Appendix 4.

[8] *Cal.* vol. 2, pp. 488, 495, 506, 510, 521-2.

[9] *Ibid.*, pp. 516.

[10] Barnes, pp. 29-31; *Cal.* vol.2, pp. 489, 540, 542.

[11] *Ibid.*, pp. 511-3, 522-3, 533, 536-8.

[12] VC/CF4/2, unpaginated.

[13] *Ibid.*; Hill, 'Estates of the Vicars Choral', pp. 24-5, 29, 37, 67-8; the 1754 survey is held at the Somerset Heritage Centre, ref. DD/CC 116014; VC/E5/3/1, VC/E3/7, 12.

[14] VC/F1/14, 15, 21, 22; for a detailed table of the college accounts for the 18th and 19th centuries, see Hill, op. cit., App. G.

[15] VC/CF4/2; VC/F1/15, 22; Warwick Rodwell, 'The Buildings of Vicars' Close' in *Wells Cathedral: A History*, ed. L.S. Colchester, p. 224.

[16] *Ibid.*; the account book (VC/F1/22) begins in 1779 and runs until 1840.

[17] Barnes, pp. 32-3; *Organs and Organists*, p. 34; R. Fiske, *English Theatre Music in the Eighteenth Century* (1973), p.639 (quoted Barnes).

[18] The system of payments to the vicars which made up their individual incomes is set out in Appendix 3.

[19] DC/CF6/15; VC/CF4/2.

[20] Barnes, pp. 33-34; DC/CF7/1.

[21] See for example, Trevor Beeson, *In Tuneful Accord: The Church Musicians* (2009), p. 17, describing St Paul's.

Chapter 6: Reform and Revival

[1] For general background to this chapter, see Philip Barrett, *Barchester: English Cathedrals in the Nineteenth Century* (1993).

[2] *The London Gazette*, 27 July 1866 (DC/E16/?....

[3] VC/CF 5/3 pp.112-3; *Parliamentary Papers: Cathedral Commission: Report, 1854*, pp. 95-105.

[4] VC/CF 5/1; Hill, 'Estates of the Vicars Choral', pp.50-1, where comparison with the increased returns after the improved management instigated by the Commissioners is illustrated. This section draws heavily on Hill's work.

[5] VC/CF5/3, July 1852, pp. 280, 301; Barnes, 'Music of Wells', pp. 43-44; Hill, pp. 47-50.

[6] VC/CF 5/3, pp. 122 ff.

[7] VC/CF5/3 pp. 408, 433-43, 451-6; VC/CF5/4, p. 1.

[8] VC/CF 5/3, pp. 512, 516, 527-33, 554, 559.

[9] DC/CF 7/4, pp. 281-2.

[10] *Ibid.*, pp. 37, 363, 368; DC/CF 7/5, pp. 37-55 passim, 68-70; DC/CF 7/6, p. 52; VC/CF 5/3, pp. 491-3.

[11] DC/CF 7/5, pp.25, 46-9, 56-74 passim, 203, 207; VC/CF 5/3 pp. 474-9, 498-503; for the text of the college oath, see Appendix 1.

[12] DC/CF 7/5, p. 85; DC/CF 7/6 p. 148.

[13] DC/CF 7/1, pp.57, 149; DC/CF 7/2, p.355.

[14] VC/CF 5/3 pp. 387-91, 399 ff.

[15] See Warwick Rodwell & Gerard Leighton, *John Carter's Architectural Records of Wells, 1784-1808*, Somerset Record Society, vol. 92 (2006), where Plate 4 shows the cathedral from the west, including Chain Gate and, in less detail, the west end of the hall before the later alterations.

[16] VC/CF 5/3, p. 269, 348-383 passim, 416; A.C. Pugin and T.L.Walker, *History and Antiquities of the Vicars Close, Wells* (1836); J.H. Parker, *Architectural Antiquities of the City of Wells* (1866); Rodwell, 'Begun While the Black Death Raged...', p. 120.

[17] VC/CF5/3, passim, see dates concerned; E.L. Elwes, *The History of Wells Theological College* (1923) passim.

[18] Barnes, pp. 34-5; DC/CF/4/1, Chapter Acts 8 Dec 1831 and 4 Dec 1832; Alfred Angel's contract at Exeter stipulated daily rehearsals, Barrett, *Barchester* p. 387.

[19] Barnes, p. 34; DC/CF 7/4, pp. 269, 308.

[20] *Organs and Organists of Wells Cathedral*, p. 35.

[21] Barnes, p. 38; DC/CF 7/4 pp. 33, 332.

[22] Colchester, *Wells Cathedral School* (1985), p. 44; Elwes, *Theological College*, p. 24; DC/CF 7/7, pp. 299, 341.

[23] DC/CF 7/7 pp. 202,255; *Organs and Organists of Wells Cathedral*, pp. 36-7.

[24] DC/CF 7/7 pp. 239, 251, 280.

[25] DC/CF 7/4 pp. 238, 259, 293, 295, 372.

[26] VC/CF 5/3, p. 559; VC/CF5/4, pp. 2, 44-49, 78, 246.

[27] DC/CF 7/4 p. 334; DC/CF 7/6, pp. 20, 27, 308, 316, 319, 324, 332; DC/CF 7/7, pp. 202, 254.

Chapter 7: Continuity and Change

[1] VC/CF 5/4 pp. 232, 243, 253, 262, 274; DC/CF 7/8 pp.12-13.

[2] *Ibid.*, p. 44; VC/CF 5/4 pp. 274, 278, 288, 292-5.

[3] *Ibid.*, pp. 343, 358, 361, 378-383, 394, 399, 410; no copies of this early leaflet exist in the college archives.

[4] *Ibid.*, pp. 167-181, 306, 399; DC/CF 7/8 pp. 62-89 *passim*.

[5] VC/CF 5/4 pp. 414, 420, 434; DC/CF 7/8, pp. 335, 337-40.

[6] DC/CF 7/8 pp. 335, 347.

[7] *Ibid.*, pp. 347-60 passim; VC/CF 5/4 pp. 432, 450-478 passim; Appleyard survived the war and returned to his duties at Wells. He finally retired, due to increasing deafness, in 1944.

[8] VC/CF 5/5 pp. 1-43 passim, 60,83 .

[9] *Ibid.*, pp. 48-55, 80; there is no further mention of vicars' documents held elsewhere, so presumably the museums returned a negative answer. However, in 2004 a 15th century cartulary previously part of the college archive was presented to the cathedral archives by Mrs A. Duncan (VC/CF 1/2); VC/CF 5/4, p. 496; VC/CF 5/5 pp. 36.

[10] VC/CF5/4, pp. 36,39; DC/CF 7/9, pp. 3,7, 38; *Organs and Organists of Wells Cathedral*, p. 37.

[11] DC/CF 7/9, pp. 48-9, 72; VC/CF/5/5, pp. 36, 69; VC/L/3.

[12] DC/CF 7/9, p. 194; VC/HIST/11, pp. 258-9.

[13] VC/L/3.

[14] VC/CF5/5, pp. 96,106, 109,115,121; DC/CF7/9, pp. 299, 302, 305, VC/L/5,6

Appendix 1: The Vicars' Oath

[1] The oath, first in Latin and then in English, is the first entry in the earliest surviving register of the Vicars, dating from 1393 (VC/CF 1/1).

Appendix 2: The Vicars' Painting

[1] VC/CF 1/1; VC/F1/12. Even in the records of the Dean and Chapter there is apparently only one reference to a painter, and that is earlier. The Communar's accounts for 1561-2 note: 'Item paide to a painter of glossetter for writing off the X Comandementes & other thinges upon the walle with in the quier, 53s. 4d.' (DC/F1/88a, p. 129).

[2] Francis Godwin, *A Catalogue of the Bishops of England* (1601), p. 301. Godwin became a prebendary of Wells in 1585 and a residentiary canon in 1587, a post he held until 1617.

[3] H Parnell, ' A History of the Vicars Choral of Wells', unpublished ms, p. 223 (VC/HIST/11).

[4] For her report see DC/ADM 8/30.

[5] In November 1862 Mr Du Cane was allowed a sum not exceeding £5 for framing 'the painting in the Vicars' Hall' (VC/CF 5/3, p.262).

Appendix 3: The Payment of Vicars

[1] Nicholas Orme, *The Minor Clergy of Exeter Cathedral, 1300-1545* (University of Exeter Press, 1980), pp. 24, 58, 66-67.

[2] *Cal.* vol.1, p. 60.

[3] *Ibid*; 12 pence = one shilling, twenty shillings = one pound; one mark = 13s. 4d., half mark = 6s.8d.; Somerset Heritage Centre, DD/CC/B131909/16.

[4] *Cal.* vol. 1, p. 37; see also pp.18, 26.

[5] DC/F 1/33.

[6] DC/CF12/6, 12; see also Chap 4, p. 2.

[7] Barnes 'The Estates of the Vicars Choral', p. 36.

[8] VC/F 1/21.

[9] *Parliamentary Papers: Cathedral Commission: Report, 1854*, pp. 95-105; VC/CF 5/3.

Appendix 4 : The Claver Morris Lawsuit, 1725

[1] *Diary*, pp. 52, 61, 121, 123; VC/L/1; VC/CF2/244; the leases are also set out in the vicars' lease book, VC/E3/6, pp. 165, 294.

BIBLIOGRAPHY

Primary Sources

The primary sources are the archives of the Dean and Chapter of Wells (DC/) and of the College of Vicars Choral of Wells (VC/). References to individual documents are given in the notes. Parts of both archives, though primarily the former, have appeared in print in the following:

Calendar of the Documents of the Manuscripts of the Dean and Chapter of Wells Historical Manuscripts Commission, 2 vols. (1907, 1914)

Printed Primary Sources

The Register of Thomas Bekynton, Bishop of Bath and Wells, 1443-1465, ed. Sir H.C. Maxwell-Lyte and M.C.B. Dawes, pt 1, Somerset Record Society, vol. 49 (1934)

'Bishop Beckington's Statutes for the Vicars Choral' in A. Watkin (ed), *Dean Cosyn and Wells Cathedral Miscellanea*, Somerset Record Society, vol. 56 (1941)

Wells Cathedral Chapter Act Book 1663-1683, ed. D.S. Bailey, Somerset Record Society, vol. 72 (1973)

A.G. Matthews (ed), *'A Revision of John Walker's Sufferings of the Clergy during the Grand Rebellion 1642-1660'* (1948)

Crown Revenues from Somerset and Dorset, 1605, ed. Colin Brett, Somerset Record Society, vol.96 (2012)

The Diary of a West Country Physician, 1684-1726, ed. Edmund Hobhouse (1934)

Parliamentary Papers: Cathedral Commission: Report, 1854

Warwick Rodwell & Gerard Leighton, *John Carter's Architectural Records of Wells, 1784-1808*, Somerset Record Society, vol. 92, (2006)

A.C. Pugin and T.L.Walker, *History and Antiquities of the Vicars Close, Wells* (1836)

J.H. Parker, *Architectural Antiquities of the City of Wells* (1866)

Valor Ecclesiasticus, (1535, repr. 1810) vol. 1

Large numbers of cathedral records prior to 1600, including those of the college, were transcribed and translated by Linzee Colchester and while privately printed and available in the cathedral library, were not formally published. They include:

'Communars' Accounts, 1327-1600' (1984)

'Documents 1348-1600 of the Vicars Choral of Wells' (1986)

'Act Book 1541-1593 of the Vicars Choral of Wells', (1986)

'Register of the Vicars Choral of Wells, 1393 – 1534' (n.d. 1980s)

Secondary Sources
Unpublished
The following are available in the cathedral library or archives

Philip Barnes, 'The Music and Musicians of Wells Cathedral to 1859', M Mus thesis, University of Manchester, 1984

Robert G. Hill, 'The Estates of the Vicars Choral of Wells Cathedral, 1591-1866', MA Dissertation, University of Bristol. 1998

H. Parnell, ' History of the Vicars Choral', ms (n.d., 1920s) (ref. VC/Hist/11)

Published

J. Alexander and P. Binski *(eds), Age of Chivalry: Art in Plantagenet England, 1200-1400*, (Royal Academy of Arts, 1987)

Philip Barrett, *Barchester: English Cathedrals in the Nineteenth Century* (1993)

Trevor Beeson, *In Tuneful Accord: The Church Musicians* (2009)

Roger Bowers, L.S. Colchester and Anthony Crossland, *Organs and Organists of Wells Cathedral* (1998 edn.)

L.S. Colchester (ed) *Wells Cathedral: A History* (1982, repr. 1996)

L.S. Colchester, *Wells Cathedral School* (1985)

Kathleen Edwards, *The English Secular Cathedrals in the Middle Ages* (Manchester University Press, 2nd edn., 1967)

E.L. Elwes, *The History of Wells Theological College* (1923)

R. Fiske, *English Theatre Music in the Eighteenth Century* (Oxford, 1973)

Francis Godwin, *A Catalogue of the Bishops of England* (1601)

Richard Hall and David Stocker (eds.), *Vicars Choral at English Cathedrals: History, Architecture and Archaeology* (Oxford, 2005), particularly Warwick Rodwell with Frances Neale, " 'Begun while the Black Death Raged...': The Vicars Close at Wells", pp. 112-137

Frank Harrison, *Music in Medieval Britain* (1958)

Frederick Harrison, *Life in a Medieval College: The Story of the Vicars Choral of York Minster* (1952)

Peter le Huray, *Music and the Reformation in England, 1549-1660* (Cambridge, 1968)

E.A. Jones, 'The Silver and Pewter of the Vicars Choral at Wells', *Burlington Magazine* (Apr. 1936)

Stamford E. Lehmberg, *The Reformation of Cathedrals: Cathedrals in English Society, 1485-1603* (Princeton, 1988)

Stamford E. Lehmberg, *Cathedrals Under Siege: Cathedrals in English Society, 1600-1700* (University of Exeter Press, 1996)

David Lepine, *A Brotherhood of Canons Serving God: English Secular Cathedrals in the Middle Ages* (Woodbridge, 1995)

K. Long, *The Music of the English Church* (1972)

Anthony Nott, *Under God's Visitation: A Study of the City of Wells from the Civil War to the Restoration* (Wells, 2010)

Nicholas Orme, *The Minor Clergy of Exeter Cathedral, 1300-1545* (University of Exeter Press, 1980)

H. Parnell, *The College of Vicars Choral Wells* (Wells, 1926)

H.E. Reynolds, *Wells Cathedral: its foundation, constitutional history and statutes* (1881)

A.J.Scrase, 'John Oker:An Organist or a Dynasty?', *Somerset and Dorset Notes & Queries*, xxxv (2003)

A.J. Scrase, 'Who were the vicars choral of Wells c.1200-1380?', *Somerset Archaeological and Natural History Society*, vol. 158 (2015)

BIBLIOGRAPHY

R.V. Sellars, 'The Chantry College in the Mountroy at Wells', *Wells Natural History and Archaeology Society Report*, 1959-60

Watkins Shaw, *The Succession of Organists from c. 1538* (1991)

A. Hamilton Thompson, *The English Clergy and their Organisation in the Later Middle Ages* (Oxford University Press, 1946)

Elsa van der Zee, *Wells Cathedral: an architectural and historical guide* (2012)

INDEX

A

Abbott, Edward, precentor, 54
Abram, Mr, schoolmaster, 98
Allen, Richard, 57
Angel, Alfred, organist, 95-6
Anne, Queen, 26
Appleyard, David, vicar, 107-8
Aris, Eldridge, vicar, 67
Armitage Robinson, Joseph, dean,
  104, 109, 114
Arundel, Thomas, Archbishop, 22
Asquith, Fergus, vicar, 102, 110
Atkins, William, vicar
Axbridge, 42
Axminster, John, vicar, 19
Awman, Robert, vicar, organist, 40
Aylworthe, John, 37, 120

B

Bacon, James, virger, 74
Ball, Joseph, vicar, 92
Baron, William, vicar, 35
Barlow, William, bishop, 40
Barrett, David, 59
Batcombe, 57
Bath, 1, 2,
  Abbey, 36
Bath & Wells, diocese of, 1
Bathurst, Ralph, dean, 70, 76, 77
Baylie, John, Dr., 64
Beauchamp, John, Revd, vicar, 87,
  92, 100
Bekynton, Thomas, bishop, 17, 19,
  22, 26-9, 31, 83, 100, 117
       John, vicar, 23
Bell, Thomas, 26
Benford, Augustin, vicar, 64
Berkeley, Gilbert, bishop, 47

Berrow, 68
Bevin, Elway, vicar, 45
Bingley, William, 71
Birch, James, 75, 100
Bisse, James, canon, 46, 48
  Philip, canon, 43
Black Death, 15-16
Bohun, Reginald de, bishop, 45
Boyfield, William, vicar, 21
Braddon, John, vicar, 35
Bramston, Richard, organist, 33-4
Bray [F.W.], clerk of works, 109
Brere, Richard, vicar, 20
Brether, John, vicar, 10
Bridgewater, 58
  John, prebendary, 47
Bristol, 41, 64
    Hospital of St Mark, 34
    St Augustine's Abbey / cathedral
    34, 45, 88, 99
Broderip, John, organist, 72-3, 78
  Edmund, 73
  John, 73
  Martha, 73
  William, vicar, 70
Brown, Nathaniel, vicar, 67
Browne, John, organist, 62, 64
Bruges, 45
Bruton Priory, 67
Bubwith, Nicholas, bishop, 24
Buche, Alice, 7
    Luke, 7
Buck, Percy, organist, 99
Buckle, Edmund, architect, 103-4
Buckler, John, 92
Burges, William, 93
  Cornelius, Dr., 59
Burland, John, 69

Burnel, Walter, vicar, 8
Burnham, 70
Burr, Joseph, Revd, vicar, 100
Byrd, William, 42

C
Canterbury cathedral, 81
Cardmaker, John, canon, 41
Carter, John, 92
Catour, Robert, Sr., vicar, 27-8, 31
                Jr., vicar, 31
Cecil, William, 42
Cerde, John de, vicar, 8
Chapel Royal, 30, 33, 43, 45, 65
Charles I, 55
Charles II, 61, 65
Cheddar, 29, 39, 59-60, 67, 75, 83
Chedzoy, 58
Cherlton, William de, 12
Chilterne, 7
Chichester cathedral, 1, 36
Church, Mrs E.M., 96
Church Commission, 111-4, 122
Clarke, Mary, 54
Clawsy, John, organist, 33
Clerke, John, vicar, 44
Cleve, John, vicar, 24
Clun, Francis, vicar, 54
      William, vicar, 54
Coke, John, 55
Commission for Woods and Forests, 58, 92
Committee for Compounding, 58
           Sequestrations, 58
Congresbury, 14, 26,
Cooper, John, vicar, 65
      Thomas, sacrist, 69
Corne, Agnes, 54
John, vicar, 54
Cosyn, William, dean, 17

Creyghton, Frideswide, 66
    Robert, dean & bishop, 61, 70
    Robert, Jr., precentor, 66, 70-1, 72, 75, 124-5
           Robert, Jr, schoolmaster, 70
Cromwell, Thomas, dean, 36
Croscombe, 75
Curle, Walter, bishop, 56
    wife of, 56

D
Dale, Valentine, dean, 43
Davies, Edmund, steward, 84, 93-4
        Thomas, Rev'd., organist, 99, 106
Defoe, Daniel, 72
Dewbery, James, vicar, 61
Dinder, 32, 75
Douai, 47
Dowthwaite, Nicholas, 64
Drayton, William, vicar, 88-9, 105
Du Cane, Arthur, Revd, vicar, 99
Dudcot, William, vicar, 23
Dulcote, 62, 72, 75, 77
Durham cathedral, 81

E
Ecclesiastical Commission, 81, 84, 91, 92, 94, 98, 103-4, 110, 113, 123
Eden, Rbt, Lord Auckland, bishop, 85
Edward I, 7
Edward III, 14
Edward VI, 38, 41
Edwardes, Richard, 42
Elizabeth, Queen, 41-2, 44, 48, 117
Elwes, Mr, 98
Ely cathedral, 81
Erdesleygh, Philip, vicar, 20
Erghum, Ralph, bishop, 37
Eton College, 27
Evans, Richard, vicar, 45

Evans, William, organist, 72-3,
Everat (Everett), Robert, vicar, 47
Everett, Thomas, vicar, 46
Exchequer, Barons of, 58, 61
Exeter cathedral, 1, 5, 32, 39, 45, 65, 95

F
Farre, ..., chorister, 34
Ferror, Stephen, 20
Fido, John, vicar, 44-5
Fisher, Thomas, vicar, 45
Fletcher, Silas, vicar, 84, 85, 101
Foster, Aaron, Revd., vicar, 77, 78, 87
        Samuel, vicar, 84
        , ..., steward, 100
Frances, Gilbert, vicar, 35
Freemasons, 103, 109
Fry, Mrs, caretaker, 104
Fynche, William, bishop of Taunton, 41

G
George, John, organist, 72
German, Thomas, vicar, 19,
Gibson, John, vicar, 43
Glastonbury Museum, 110
Gleaves, Joseph, vicar, 85-6, 88-9
Gloucester cathedral, 41, 98
Gloucestershire, 6
Godelee, Hamelin, 12
        John, dean, 12-14
Godwin, Francis, canon, 51, 117
Godwyn, Thomas, bishop, 48
Graye, John, vicar, 19
Greene, Gabriel, 65
Greenwood, ..., vicar, 100
Grey, Ford, Lord Grey of Warke, 66
Gybbes, Walter, vicar, 19
Gye, John, vicar, 34

H
Halston, John, vicar, 19
Harewell, John, bishop, 26
Harman, John, vicar, 46
Harptree, Luke de, vicar, 9
Harris, John, organbuilder, 74
Haselshawe, Walter de, bishop, 10
Hawes, Thomas, Revd., vicar, 85
Henry VI, 27
Henry VIII, 36, 38
Herbert, John, dean, 48
Hereford cathedral, 1, 41, 88
Hervey, Lord Arthur, bishop, 86
Hill, Samuel, 69
Hill, William, vicar, 68
Hippesley, Edmund, 85, 87
Hodge, Robert, organist, 65
Hodgkinson, Albert, vicar, 111
Hodgson, Walter, Revd., vicar, 107
Holt, Thomas, chancellor, 66
Holy Land, 8
Hooper, George, bishop, 125
Hotham, Adam de, canon, 14
Hoyland, William de, vicar, 8-9
Hughes, Richard, Revd., vicar, 74
Huish, John, canon, 26, 39
Hulett, John, vicar, 44
Hulle, Richard, vicar, 20-1
Walter de, vicar, 9
Hungerford, Lady, 29
Hunt, Richard, vicar (1770), 77
Hygons, Richard, vicar, 32-33

I
Ine, king of Wessex, 1
Irish, Elizabeth, 126

J
Jackson, John, organist, 64-5, 70
James I, 53

James II, 65
Jefferies, Judge, 66
       Matthew, vicar, 45-6
Jerrard, Mr, vicar, 92
Jocelin of Wells, bishop, 5, 6, 119
Johnson, Edward, vicar, 67
Josce, daughter of, 8

K

Kaynell, Christine, 29
      John, 29
Kearton, Joseph, vicar, 86-7, 90
Ken, Thomas, bishop, 65
Kennion, George Wyndham, bishop,
  104
Kymer, William, Revd. Vicar, 74
Kidder, Richard, bishop, 71
      daughter of, 71
Kingstone, 26, 39, 75, 83, 84

L

Lane, Betty, housekeeper, 75
Simon, vicar, 46
Lanfranc, archbishop, 1
Laud, William, archbishop, 55-7
Lavington, Charles, organist, 96-7
Layng, Dr, 125
Lewes, Francis, chorister, 56
Lichfield cathedral, 1
Lincoln cathedral, 1, 12
Lincolnshire, 6
Linley, Thomas, composer, 78
London, Drury Lane Theatre, 78
St Paul's cathedral, 1, 12, 41, 42, 45
Smithfield, 41
    Tower of, 58, 79
    University of, 99
    V & A Museum, 109-110
Lyde, William, organist, 40-1, 44
Lye, Henry Leigh, vicar, 98

M

Maldon, Henry, dean, 114
Marchia, William de, bishop, 7
Martock, 39, 75
Martyn, Henry, 24
Mary, Queen, 41
Mason, Richard, vicar, 53
Menyman, John, vicar & canon, 31, 33
Merriman, William, vicar, 89, 101-2
Millard, Joseph, vicar, 72
Miller, John, vicar, 107-8
Mills, Henry, schoolmaster, 70
Monmouth, James, duke of, 66
Moody, C.H., organist, 99
Morris, Claver, Dr., 69, 71, 109, 124-6
      Elizabeth, 69
Mowrie, Anthony, vicar, 61

N

Nailer, Matthew, vicar, 47
Newton Plecy, manor of, 29, 30, 39,
  60, 75
Nicholson, Sir Charles, architect, 109
Nooth, James, vicar, 70
North Petherton, 29
Nottinghamshire, 6

O

Okeover (Oker), John, organist, 54-5,
  58, 61-2
Oker, George, chorister, 56
    John, chorister, 62
    Mary, 62
Orum, John, vicar, 20
Oxford, 31

P

Palmer, Revd., schoolmaster, 98
Parfitt, James, vicar, 78, 85
Peter, organist, 78

Parker, John Henry, 93
Parliament, acts of, 37, 69, 80-1, 86, 108
        Survey, 60, 62
Parnell, Hugh, Revd, vicar, 111, 114
Parry, Robert, organist, 78
Parsons, William, organist, 40
Partridge, Harry, vicar, 113
Paston, Henry, vicar, 35
Pedewell, John, canon, 29
        John, vicar, 29
Pencriz, Richard de, vicar, 9
Pennard, 75
Perkins, Dodd, organist, 78-9, 95
       William, organist, 78-9, 95-7
Perlee, Robert, canon, 22
Perry, Farwell, vicar, 67-8
Phear, Nurse, 76
Piers, William, bishop, 57, 61, 62,
       William, jr., 65
Pitcher, John, chorister, 43-4
Plummer, Joan, 46
Polsham, 75
Pomeroy, Richard, vicar, 35
Pontesbury, Nicholas, 26
Poore, Richard, bishop of Salisbury, 2
Pope, Henry, vicar, 56, 60
       Joan, 56-7
Popham, Alexander, Col., 57
Poulet, Francis, 124-5
Praule, Geoffrey de, vicar, 9
Privy Council, 52
Pugin, Augustus, sr. & jr., 93
Purcell, Henry, 65

Q
Queen Anne's Bounty, 104

R
Raleigh, Walter, kt., 46
Raleigh, dean, 58-9, 61

Ralph of Shrewsbury, bishop, 11, 14
  19, 25, 29, 51, 77, 117, 121
Reade, James, vicar, 53
Reformation, 5, 36 ff.
Richard II, 26
Ripon cathedral, 99
Revett, Timothy, canon, 54
Robert of Lewes, bishop, 2
Rogers, George, vicar, 68
       Mary, 68
Rolle, Edward, vicar, 92
Rome, 5, 36
Royal Commission, 81
Rumsey, Thomas, vicar, 47

S
Salisbury cathedral, 1, 4, 32, 39, 46, 71, 88
Sarum Customary/Use/Ordinal, 2-4
Sedgemoor, battle of, 66
Sharp, Henry, kt., 114
Sherborne, diocese of
Shipham, manor of, 29
Slade, Mr, 125
Smith, John, vicar, 34, 35
       Notary public, 39
Society of Antiquaries of London, 92
Somerset, 6
Stafford, John, bishop, 27
Standish, Francis, vicar, 59, 61, 63
Sugar, Hugh, Dr, canon, 30
Sun Fire Office, 95
Swansee, Alice, 16
       Philip, 16
Swarbrick, Thomas, 71, 74
Symonds, Martin, vicar

T
Tailer, Walter, vicar, 54
Tallis, Thomas, 42
Tanner, Avice, 8

David, 8
Tawswell, William, vicar, 46
Taylor, Arthur, vicar, 101, 106-8
John, vicar, 45
Teight, Joan, 46
Thomas, Vicars' cook
Tottensis, Geoffrey de, vicar, 9
Tregodek, John, vicar, 19
Trustees for the Maintenance of
  Ministers, 61
Trycer, Robert, vicar, 43
Turle, James, 96
Turner, William, dean, 40

U
Urchisfont, Simon, vicar, 20

V
Vagele, Walter, vicar, 31
Vicars Choral
  concubines of, 8, 10, 12, 46
  portrait of, 51, 117-8
  Regulations/Statutes of, 10-11, 17,
    51, 67-8, 85-6, 91, 104, 108
  wives of, 38, 40, 41, 42, 45, 56,
    68, 85-6
  Vicars' Chapel, 25, 41, 94
  Vicars' Close, 16-18, 25-6, 62-3, 76,
    77, 83, 85-7, 94, 124-6
  Vicars' Hall, 15-16, 24, 28, 36, 64,
    71, 76, 93, 94, 103-4, 109
Vesey, Hugh, vicar, 35

W
Walkley, Anthony, vicar, 71
Wallis, Robert, Dr, vicar, 91, 100, 101
Wansford, John, canon, 23
Wanstrow, 62
Ward, Alexander, vicar, 41
Webb, Thomas, 72

Wedmore, 119
  Baggelegh wood, 8
Weekes, John, vicar, 43
Wellesley, 75
Wellesley, Elizabeth, 17
  John, kt., 17
Wells Archaeological Society, 104
Wells, Cathedral
  altars, 6
  Anglo-Saxon cathedral 1
  Camery, 12
  canonical hours, 3, 10, 38
  Chain Gate, 28-9, 100
  Chancellor, 2-4, 101, 106
  chantries, 7, 120
  chapels,
  Chapter House, 2, 28, 67, 101, 106
  choristers, 6, 27, 32, 56, 98
  Choristers' House, 27, 33, see also
    Organist's House
  Grammar School, 6, 27, 32, 40, 42, 98
  Lady Chapel, 4, 31-3, 57, 61, 67, 94
  Lady Chapel by the Cloister, 7, 37
  Library, 57, 70, 94
  organ, 4, 30-1, 61, 98
  Organist's House, 95, 97
  Palm Churchyard, 37, 74
  Penniless Porch, 95
  Precentor, 2-3, 99, 106
  schoolmaster, 6, 27-8
  Succentor, 4
  Sub-dean, 4
  Treasurer, 2-3
Wells Cathedral School, 6, 95, 98
Wells, City of
  almshouses, 39,59
  Archdeacon's House, 95
  Canon Grange, manor of, 70
  Cathedral Green, 12, 14
  Cedars, The, 95

Chamberlain Street, 39, 75,
Christopher Inn, 26, 39, 75, 83
College Lane, 63, 72, 124
East Walls, 75
Gas Light Co., 95
Grammar School, 98
Grope Lane, 75
High Street, 26, 39, 75
Howsel Lane, 39,
Middle School, 98
Mitre Inn, 65
Moniers Lane, 24
Monterey (Monteroy, Mount Roy,
    Montrey), 22, 37, 75
Museum, 98, 110
North Liberty, 14, 63
Paving and Lighting
Commissioners, 95
Rib, The, 12, 95
Sadler Street, 12
St Andrew's Street, 60, 109, 124
St Cuthbert's church, 9, 31, 35, 59
Southover, 26, 39, 75
Tor Lane, 34, 75
Tucker Street, 75
Wells Theological College, 94-5,
    98, 104, 114
Welsh, John, vicar, 78
        Thomas, chorister, 78
Westminster Abbey, 58, 96
White, Helen, 118
White, Robert, vicar, 32
Whitgift, John, archbishop, 52
Whiting, William, 60
Whyte, John, 39
Wicks, Thomas, vicar, 85-6, 105
Williams, James, sacrist,
Willis, Henry, 98
Winchcombe, Henry, vicar, 64
Winchester cathedral, 81

College, 27
Windsor, St George's Chapel, 84
Winscombe, 15, 30
Wiseman, John, vicar, 86-7, 89-90
Witherell, John, steward, 75
Wiveliscombe, 15
Wookey, 14, 26
Worcester cathedral, 88
Worcestre, William, 26
World War One, 107

Y
Yarrow, Robert, vicar, 53
Young, Robert, schoolmaster, 98
York Minster, 1, 12, 32, 45